Designing Supply Chains for New Product Development

Designing Supply Chains for New Product Development

Antonio Arreola-Risa and Barry Keys

businessexpert
Press

First published in 2013 by
Business Expert Press, LLC
222 East 46th Street, New York, NY 10017
www.businessexpertpress.com

ISBN-13: 978-1-60649-395-3 (paperback)
ISBN-13: 978-1-60649-396-0 (e-book)

Business Expert Press Supply and Operations Management Collection

Collection ISSN: 2156-8189 (print)
Collection ISSN: 2156-8200 (electronic)

Cover and interior design by Exeter Premedia Services Private Ltd.,
Chennai, India

First edition: 2013

10 9 8 7 6 5 4 3 2 1

Printed in the United States of America.

Abstract

Research and development (R&D) supply chains are oftentimes designed without the process discipline and rigor that typically characterize the development of products emerging from R&D programs. As such, this text attempts to fill a gap experienced by everyday supply chain practitioners involved in research and new product development, who are migrating their products to full commercialization, as well as to help decision makers looking to improve the overall effectiveness and efficiency of their supply chain.

When new products are developed, a significant divide typically emerges when trying to commercialize the product while attempting to meet project demands for cost, schedule, and quality. Simply put, in many cases the supply chains developed to accomplish R&D functions are usually woefully inadequate to meet the demands of large-scale commercial applications.

This book recounts the real-world work efforts, rigor, and discipline used to transition from a supply chain supporting R&D functions to a world-class supply chain capable of supporting a multibillion-dollar hydrocarbon recovery project.

Keywords

supply chain, research and development, new product development, best-in-class, make versus buy, risk modeling, inventory control, intellectual property, total cost of ownership, decision framing and analysis.

Contents

Acknowledgments

No book is complete without recognizing the help and support of others. We dedicate this book to them.

To my wife Cecivón and my children Cecivonita, Tony, Maui, and Alex. You were my source of inspiration. To my esteemed colleague Dr. Bill Stein for your insightful input and invaluable critical thinking. And to my now friend Barry Keys for inviting me to work with him on the supply-chain design project.

Tony Arreola-Risa

To my wife, Karla, and daughters Alyx and Andi, thank you so much for being there for me. To my teammates, of which there were many, and I can only name a few; Greg, Susan, Jeremy, Adam, Alan, Michael, Dave, Sonja, Jorge, Jaime, Bob, Don, Dr. John, Wade, Joe, Guy, Jack, Joel, you guys were the best and I would do it all over again with you. Dr. Tony, a special thank you for all that you have done, your friendship especially. There were many others who we touched and that we were touched by, and I thank you.

Barry Keys

We are also grateful to Dr. Lawrence Di Paolo, who read many drafts of the book and provided us with many recommendations for improvement. Last but not least, we want to thank the folks at Business Expert Press because without them, this book would still be locked in our minds, and our experiences would have never been shared with a large audience.

Tony Arreola-Risa and Barry Keys

Foreword

Why this book? When this project first started, it seemed to be a relatively simple idea to build a supply chain to support commercialization of a product that had been built and tested by research and development personnel. As a Fortune 500 company engaged in world-wide operations, a supply department effectively meeting the company's needs, and the prevailing wisdom that suppliers would be "knocking at our door" to be part of the billion-dollar plus project we were planning, setting up the supply chain for the new product would appear to be a cake-walk. Nothing could have been further from the truth.

Unfortunately, there did not seem to be a "Supply Chain 101" book that met our needs. After extensive research of the existing literature, we came to the following conclusions: (1) currently, there has been no significant effort to publicly document the supply chain development effort that needs to occur when trying to move from new product development to full-scale commercialization, and (2) if companies performing new product development on the scale that we were planning were developing their associated supply chains in parallel, they were keeping it a secret ostensibly to maintain competitive advantage in the marketplace.

There is significant documentation regarding supply chain optimization, supply chain redesign, supply chain "this" and supply chain "that," but what about the original thought that goes into putting a new supply chain together? Where does that body of knowledge reside? This book is a small attempt to document the process and the discipline, in a relatively straightforward manner, and to hopefully make life just a bit easier for the person who has been tasked with "developing a world-class supply chain for this brand-new product, which will change the world."

Introduction

Research and development (R&D) supply chains are often times developed without the process discipline and rigor that typically characterize the development of products emerging from R&D programs. As such, this text attempts to fill a gap experienced by everyday supply chain practitioners involved in research and new product development, who are migrating their products to full commercialization, as well as to help anyone looking to improve the overall effectiveness and efficiency of their supply chain.

When new products are developed, a significant divide typically emerges when trying to commercialize the product while simultaneously attempting to meet project demands for cost, schedule, and quality. Simply put, in many cases the supply chains developed to accomplish R&D functions are usually woefully inadequate to meet the demands of large-scale commercial applications.

This book recounts the real-world work efforts, rigor, and discipline used to transition from a supply chain supporting R&D functions to a world-class supply chain capable of supporting a multi-billion dollar hydrocarbon recovery project. Specifically, the book describes supply chain evaluation techniques, processes, and program initiatives developed and used by a project team over a four-year period, to commercialize a newly developed "down-hole" tool specifically created to aid hydrocarbon recovery from oil shale and heavy oil reservoirs. While the cost of the tool itself was in fact a relatively small portion of the proposed multi-billion dollar oil and gas recovery project, it had a few "wrinkles." First of all, it required the use of what the average person may view as copious amounts of precious metals. Second, the unit cost for the experimental models, material only, was running on the order of $250,000. Third, there were components in the tool that were extremely difficult and expensive to manufacture. Fourth, there were heavy intellectual property investments in materials, design, assembly, and deployment. Fifth, the product had to survive the harsh, down-hole operating conditions for a minimum of five years with no failures. Sixth, the tool design was constantly being modified as results from field trials were incorporated into the design while at the same time the work to establish a supply chain was being performed. Last but not least, once the tool was in the ground, there was little to no hope of it ever being recovered, much less recycled, with any sort of positive economic benefit. Sorry, we should have said there were a few, BIG, wrinkles.

As stated, the tool was a relatively small portion of a multi-billion dollar oil and gas recovery project on a cost per unit basis; however, failure of the tool had tremendous implications to overall project success. At a minimum, the *total* tool cost, labor, and material needed to be reduced by 50% from the research and development *material only* costs. The technology was difficult to manufacture, was subject to significant engineering design changes, and the "know-how" for its design, configuration, manufacturing, assembly, and deployment was highly proprietary and (hopefully) well-protected via patents.

Trying to get something to work in R&D and then mass-producing it in a way that the mass-produced product results are acceptable is extremely difficult and cannot be underestimated. As many in the R&D community would emphatically echo, "there are about 10,000 things that we know will not work." The rigor and discipline required for supply chain development in R&D, in many cases, pales in comparison to the effort required in developing a supply chain required to support mass production. After all, R&D is R&D and is never expected to make a profit. It is a cost of doing business. The supply chain development efforts of R&D should really remind one of a "hunter-gatherer"-type approach. Ideas get floated about, some are selected via some sort of internal screening process, investigations are performed to determine capabilities of many different suppliers in meeting requirements, and purchase orders are issued to those suppliers that can best meet the needs, not only from a technology point of view, but also from a scheduling and product quality point of view.

Sometimes, the R&D budget may end up funding capital expansions at supplier locations. Usually, the supplier has only a general idea of what is supposed to be accomplished but is willing to work with the client if the following general conditions can be met:

1. What is being asked is not too much of a stretch from what the supplier is presently doing.
2. What the client wants done will not significantly interfere with supplier production schedules.
3. The funding is appropriate.
4. The client must specify exactly what is wanted and may not observe or participate in any of the processes or procedures that are used to meet the requirements.
5. There may or may not be sharing in any sort of "new" intellectual property that is developed as the product or component that is being made undergoes various improvements.

When the decision was taken to start "commercializing" this new tool emerging out of R&D, particularly in an organization that was not accustomed to new product development, a whole new set of issues also came into existence. A new team was brought in to start developing the commercial aspects of the product (and the new team did not know anything!). The existing supply chain that had faithfully served the R&D community was found to be woefully inadequate for the scope of the intended overall project; expectations regarding tool cost reductions, manufacturing times, quality, supplier engagement, and so on, were unrealistically high, and the level of effort required to start the overall project on-time was underestimated. So, while life was already difficult in trying to develop a tool that would survive the down-hole environment, a whole new level of complexity was added when the decision was made to develop its associated supply chain in parallel. With these things in mind, let's go ahead and get started.

CHAPTER 1

Supplier Landscape

What Are We Talking About
and How Much Do We Need?

The first order of business is figuring out how much "stuff" you are going to need to meet your requirements. In this case, we mentioned earlier that the average person would view our requirements for precious metals as huge. That said, there may be some concerns in your company regarding what impact your requirements may have on world markets. A related and also very important issue is, if it can be determined whether or not any correlations exist between your material requirements and the financial markets. How would your requirements affect the volatility of the base materials? Are there any price inelasticities in your materials? What outside factors, not associated with your project, may have significant repercussions on your project? If the material contribution of your requirements is added to the material contributions of other related aspects of the project, would the total material requirements of the entire project have any sort of impact on world commodity markets? How do regulatory policies, tariffs, anti-dumping legislation, and other global supply-chain issues impact your decisions with regard to how one develops the supporting supply chain?

With these questions in mind, it is usually helpful to engage a consultant or two to assist in researching these questions. While most commodity information is public, there are a couple of issues to consider:

1. How much time do you, as the commercial development person, have to perform the research?
2. Do you have the correct skill sets on hand to perform the research?
3. Does your organization have a tendency or inclination toward a concept that might be called "proof by consultant"?
4. Will your results be accepted without independent corroboration by another organization?

The first two issues were relatively straightforward. Literally hundreds of hours were spent researching basic raw materials and determining any positive or negative correlations with the financial markets. We simply did not have the time to do it ourselves; more importantly, we did not have the skill sets on staff required to perform this sort of a study. The third issue was a bit more problematic. In this case, the company had developed a culture of "proof by consultant." The thought here is that while one may have the requisite skills, knowledge, abilities, and talents to meet roles and responsibilities, sometimes there are aspects of your roles and responsibilities that you may simply not be an expert in, or have working knowledge of, that can be brought to bear on the question. In our case, this culture became burdensome as there were times when even some of the most fundamental issues regarding suppliers and commodities were challenged, and while the staff worked to provide good answers to questions, the "answers" were not fully accepted unless they were independently corroborated by consultants, and even then, those consultants sometimes needed to be extremely well-regarded in the marketplace and by corporate headquarters. It is up to you as the practitioner to figure out if this situation exists and working in advance to clearly identify management's expectations with respect to consultant use and acceptance of results.

Moving back to the situation with which we were presented, the tool used large quantities of copper and stainless steel; therefore, there was significant concern regarding just how much impact our requirements would have on prices for copper, nickel, and any of the constituent components of stainless steel. There was also a concern regarding positive correlations between oil prices and commodity markets, and price fluctuations with respect to global events. The concern at one point was so great that some thought that the only way to secure raw materials would be to purchase mines and ore processing companies. While this may seem to be a bit grandiose, it wasn't until the fundamental research was performed that insight could be gained into these questions.

So, the first order of business was to select a well-regarded consultant to perform the necessary research. After defining the scope of work and time frame for work completion, it was then extremely important to monitor progress and manage upward (i.e., keep management up to date—no surprises) with respect to intermediate results of the research and to keep the study on track. In our case, we disassembled the product to the base commodity materials, determined quantities per unit, multiplied by number of units per year, and then multiplied by the life of the project. This was the easy part. The hard part was in answering questions with respect to global market demand for these same raw materials over the life of the project.

Study Results

In our case, given the scope of the project, there would be little to no impact on global commodities for mass production of the new tool. When combined with the raw material aspects of the other programs associated with the overall project (drilling, electrical, instrumentation, etc.), there was still no significant impact. Given the global events occurring at the time, and those anticipated to come, we were finally convinced that we would not be required to purchase any mines or ore processing companies, or backwardly integrate into any of these industries, even if we were to consider performing several projects simultaneously. Exhibit 1-1 shows examples of study results.

Compared to the world production, the project represented too small of a demand to achieve any economies of scale. In addition, while there was minimal risk of vertical market failure, we needed to realize that the primary metals mining industry is a capital-intensive and cyclical business subject to volatile commodities markets and that other strategies would need to be developed to mitigate supply-chain material risks.

Exhibit 1-1. Example of Study Results for Material Requirements

Commodity	Global production (metric tons)	Product material requirements for a single project as a percentage of global production	Product material requirements for several projects as a percentage of global production	Total project material requirements for a single project as a percentage of global production
Carbon Steel	878,000,000	<0.1	<1	<0.1
Stainless Steel	24,000,000	<0.1	<5	<0.5
Copper	13,600,000	<0.2	<5	<0.5
Nickel	1,340,000	<0.2	<5	<0.5
Chromium	4,940,000	<0.1	<5	<0.5
Molybdenum	129,000	<0.1	<1	<0.5
Tungsten	59,100	<0.1	<5	<0.5
Cobalt	40,300	<0.2	<5	<0.5
Niobium	32,800	<0.1	<1	<0.5

Developing from the results of the above studies, a new series of questions regarding oil and metal price correlations were identified. These questions were a bit more difficult to answer. In some cases, depending on the time frame that was examined, there appeared to be positive correlations between energy prices and commodities prices, particularly when prices were corrected by producer price index values for the time frame, but it was extremely difficult to make any sense out of them. For periods less than 10 years, there was little statistically significant correlation. For long periods, that is, over 30 years, there was statistically significant correlation (see Exhibit 1-2). The reasons for this appeared to be twofold:

1. historical inflation data (i.e., using the producer price index) are really just an estimate and cannot be uniformly applied across all industry sectors;
2. contemporary inflation reports do not exclude effects caused by changes in energy prices.

The bottom line here is that one was trying to make well-educated guesses of data that are difficult to interpret correctly and that further information was required.

Aggravating the situation regarding energy prices was an apparent inelasticity associated with copper and nickel pricing. Since the tool required a fairly significant amount of copper and nickel, our concern was that project economics would suffer significant negative impact, should large price swings occur with these two commodities. We discovered that small perturbations in supply caused large price swings with resultant spikes in copper and nickel prices being several times their base production cost. In addition, global economic growth during this period of time served to fuel the perception of increased oil prices driving increased commodity prices.

Significant study was devoted to this area, and our conclusions were that while oil prices and metal prices could be correlated to singular events, they could not be directly correlated to each other. Specifically, since our project required extensive use of stainless steel, nickel commodity prices were of great interest to us. The steady rise in the world production, coupled with a steady US demand, made it appear that the cost of nickel was decreasing. However, small mismatches in supply and demand caused large perturbations in price, not production and consumption. Changing

Exhibit 1-2. Correlation Between Oil and Metals Prices (30 years) (correlations in bold font are statistically significant)

	Year	Crude Oil	Steel	Nickel	Copper	Chrome	Moly	Cobalt	Tungsten	Niobium
Year	1									
Crude Oil	0.7	1								
Steel	0.83	0.81	1							
Nickel	0.7	0.6	0.66	1						
Copper	0.71	0.54	0.71	0.87	1					
Chrome	0.77	0.68	0.82	0.64	0.76	1				
Moly	0.27	0.66	0.4	0.45	0.37	0.37	1			
Cobalt	0.59	0.43	0.57	0.45	0.67	0.72	0.42	1		
Tungsten	-0.06	0.2	0.11	0.09	0.22	0.41	0.43	0.39	1	
Niobium	-0.3	0.19	-0.1	-0.11	-0.11	0.09	0.54	0.17	0.71	1

market conditions caused producers to add or mothball capacity as dictated by market conditions. For example, the run-up in nickel prices in the late 1980s was essentially caused by a depression of nickel prices from 1979–1982 due to the oil crisis (with a subsequent reduction in nickel demand) followed by a surge in stainless steel demand in 1987. As the market attempted to recover from the increased stainless steel demand, the dissolution of the Soviet Union in 1991 caused an excess of military grade nickel to be dumped onto world markets. This dumping combined with scrap stockpile sales depressed the price of nickel further. In 2000, the Chinese demand for stainless steel (~20% per year) significantly contributed to the recovery of nickel prices and essentially eliminated all excess nickel production capacity by 2004. Both nickel and copper prices continued to demonstrate this inelastic tendency during the entire time this project was under consideration. While there is little to no long-term correlation over 40 years, there is a short-term correlation between crude oil prices and nickel prices directly attributable to one-time, short-term events. No other metals exhibited this type of correlation, and there was little value in trying to predict nickel prices based on single, short-term events. Correlation existed between metals but not directly with oil. So, while a project will see short-term correlations due to singular events, it would be inappropriate to assume that the short-term correlations observed would be applicable over the entire life of the commercial project.

Do the Results Make Sense?

Therefore, after all the number crunching and intensive analysis, it is wise to take a step back and ask what is really governing the behavior of the commodities one is examining to determine existence of correlations and go back to the fundamentals. In our case, when a comparison is made between the drivers of the two industries, the following can be observed:

Oil market drivers:
1. Limited resources
2. Uneven distribution of oil deposits
3. National company controls
4. Major cartels (i.e., OPEC)
5. Major geopolitical risks

Metals markets drivers:

1. Supplies appear to be unlimited for centuries
2. Wide distribution of deposits
3. Free enterprise markets
4. Competitive markets
5. Small geopolitical risks

Analyzing the Potential Supply Base

Over a 2-year period, the team evaluated over 500 different suppliers, each with some purported ability to be a supply-chain participant. Of those suppliers, less than 5% possessed any significant measure of capability and capacity to meet mass production requirements. Evaluating these suppliers also led to some very interesting insights. The first is that, economically speaking, a suppliers market existed. Suppliers can, and did, charge what the market would bear for competing goods and services. Where the product technology was well-aligned with existing suppliers of goods and services, competitive pricing was available. Where the product technology was not well-aligned, the differences were strongly reflected in increased costs of the desired materials and their associated forms. Additionally, while the quantities of materials compared to the global commodity market were not large, they did represent significant order quantities to potential suppliers. For example, steel markets are very competitive so the likelihood of obtaining volume discounts (5% or more) became highly unlikely. Secondly, while the technology was relatively simple in concept, it was quite complex in design. Very few suppliers had the capability to deliver components, much less subassemblies, required for the final design, and none had the capacity to meet the needs of a large commercial project. Thirdly, where capability and capacity existed, it was constrained, and suppliers were generally ambivalent to our needs. In the general case, suppliers that we would have liked to utilize based on their level of involvement in serving the R&D supply chain would have become incapable of meeting the demands of their existing customer base if they were to agree to participate in supply chain for the commercial project. Without some sort of capital infusion from the firm, they would encounter production delays, lower than desired order fulfillment rates, and significant aggravation due to the ever-changing technical requirements of the tool. Given oil prices near $100/barrel, an excellent business environment, and the wide ranges of uncertainty for the commercial project timing, we were unable to make compelling arguments to suppliers for further development of their internal capability and capacity on their own. The lesson we learned, was simply that, under these market conditions, suppliers will choose to work with customers possessing hard and fast material requirements and firm dates rather than work on high potential projects with a large degree of uncertainty with respect to timing, volume, and pricing. Simply put, suppliers were *not* lining up at the door to do business with us because the level of uncertainty in our business case was too great of a risk to them.

Conclusion

In conclusion then, some key issues to focus on are:

1. How much "stuff" are we talking about?
2. Do we know where this "stuff" is already being used and can some insight be developed into the potential impact if the project moves forward?
3. Do correlations exist between singular events and/or financial markets?
4. If a singular event has a duration lasting several years, can a strategy be developed to mitigate the effects of the event and still move forward with the project?
5. Does your understanding of the fundamental drivers for the major commodities being examined make sense for the analysis results that you have obtained?
6. Can a business case be established so that suppliers are willing to become involved?
7. Are the processes and procedures, quality control, and technology requirements for the new product well-aligned with current industry providers?
8. Do the existing suppliers supporting the R&D function have the capability and capacity to be a significant participant in a mass production environment?
9. Can short-term market phenomena be incorporated into associated economic models?

CHAPTER 2

Make Versus Buy

Once there is a fair idea of what the overall material requirements are going to be, as well as of the supplier landscape, one can now move to the next level of questions. Surely some piece of this new product being invented can be made by someone else. After all, if the items presently being purchased are not already being made, then the R&D program would basically be at a standstill. Is there a way that we could get some of these suppliers to make the whole thing? Typical questions for this line of thinking include: "With the scope of our project, suppliers should be knocking at the door to help us out, and we ought to be able to farm out all of it"; "Why can't we do this elsewhere?"; "We need to keep our costs down and making things is not our core business." Perhaps you may like to add a few more.

Analyzing Leverage Points

So how do you decide? One way to sort things out is to determine where the greatest amounts of leverage are going to be obtained and in whose favor those leverages would be. Certainly if most of the leverage is heading towards your suppliers, then the next issue to consider is the manufacturing versus assembly discussion. Suppliers of commodity-type items will most likely not be too interested in supplying the final assembly for the same very reason that you may not be too interested in doing it yourself. The business case for building the final assembly for someone else simply cannot be justified. Just to be clear though, the make versus buy analysis is regarding those parts that will be made by the company and those which will be bought by the company. It also includes the entire chain of events that need to occur to produce the final product. Ultimately the decisions will be based on advantages and disadvantages for manufacturing, market structures, and the balance between flexibility and control needed by the firm.

Exhibit 2-1. Determining Balance

Decision point	Make "it" if:	Buy "it" if:
Internal Manufacturing Capability	High	Low
Internal Manufacturing Capacity	High	Low
Operational/Capital Expenditure Advantage	Internal (low-cost of capital)	Supplier (expertise, know-how, etc.)
Product Margin	High	Low
Structural Advantage	Internal (ability to pool materials, purchasing power)	Supplier (scale, location, relationship)
Number of Qualified Suppliers	Very Few (2)	Several (5)
Overall Supply Chain Costs	High Inventory and Transport Costs	Low Inventory and Transport Costs
Vertical Market Failure Risk	High	Low
Supplier Power	Suppliers have monopolistic tendencies/behaviors	Buyer has power to negotiate contracts
Intellectual Property	Difficult & Potentially Unmanageable	Relatively normal
Number of Design Changes	Frequent within existing technology	Few or none
Production Flexibility	Critical	Not Critical
Access to all Production Information	Required and supplier unable/ unwilling to provide	Not required/ necessary
Control Over Manufacturing	Critical for differentiation and sustaining competitive advantage	Not Critical
Long-term Strategic Importance	High	Low

Balance

So just what are the leverage points that should be considered? If one can picture a "balance beam" in one's mind, then we will start constructing a decision framework as outlined in Exhibit 2-1.

Initial Determination of Supplier Relationships

As mentioned, a matrix can be built to perform a qualitative analysis of the final product and, using this framework, to identify leverage points in three specific areas: raw materials, intermediate processing/sub-assembly

formation, and final processing/assembly. The idea here is that by breaking the final product down into three basic formation steps, and using
the matrix in Exhibit 2-1, further insight may be gained into leverage
points between the firm and prospective suppliers. In our particular case,
we broke down the final assembly into six major sub-assemblies, with no
regard to the production processes or manufacturing requirements associated with each sub-assembly. Using the balance beam approach from
Exhibit 2-1, the resultant matrix revealed that in all cases but one, we
should simply purchase the sub-assembly from a supplier. In the single
case that stood out, we should still purchase the sub-assembly, but we
needed to institute very tight controls around intellectual property protection and control over manufacturing. The analysis for the final assembly,
on the other hand, revealed that the firm should take a "make" decision.

By analyzing the make versus buy decision within this overall framework, and in consideration of manufacturing versus assembly as discussed
at the end of this chapter, it should become clear that a "buy" decision
should be taken, in the general case, if suppliers have scale and expert
advantages over the firm as there is little value in the firm developing
the associated know-how. Where tight process controls and quality assurance and control information will be required, intellectual property needs
to be protected, and/or supplier qualification efforts are proving to be
extremely difficult to perform, significant consideration should be given
toward taking appropriate "make" decisions, perhaps starting in a few of
the intermediate processing steps, but certainly in those critical areas of
final assembly and processing.

Regarding "buy" decisions, it is important to determine the significance of the impact a supplier would have on the organization, should they
not be able to meet the customer's needs. To understand the impact just a
bit better, we developed the matrix shown in Exhibit 2-2 (which resembles
Kraljic's matrix), to identify those suppliers that we needed to carefully
manage our relationship with. The idea behind this matrix was to first
determine the significance of the impact, and then using these results, place
the suppliers into one of four different relationship categories as follows.

1. **Bottleneck:** this category was characterized as being a non-strategic
   technical relationship, where complex specifications requiring

Exhibit 2-2. Supplier Relationship Categories

Bottleneck Non-strategic technical	Critical Strategic technical strategic service
• Complex specifications requiring complex manufacturing or service process • Few alternative sources of supply • Big impact on operations or maintenance • New technology or untested process	• Critical to profitability and operations • Few qualified sources of supply • Large expenditures • Design and quality critical • Complex and/or rigid specifications • Requires significant skill
Routine Non-strategic commodity non-strategic service	Leverage Strategic commodity
• Many alternative products and services • Many sources of supply • Low value small individual transactions • Everyday use unspecified items • Anyone could buy it	• High expenditures, commodity items • Large market capacity, sample inventories • Many alternate product and services • Many qualified sources of supply • Market and price sensitive

complex manufacturing or service requirements existed and there were only a few suppliers. The services or products required would have a significant impact on either operations or maintenance, and/ or the supplier was developing a new technology or had untested/ unproven processes. Obviously, this was not a supply relationship that was highly desirable.

2. **Critical:** this category could represent either a strategic technical product or service that was critical to the profitability and operations of the firm. A few qualified suppliers existed, and fairly large expenditures would occur with each supplier; design and quality control requirements were very high and were accompanied by complex and rigid specifications, and the service or product required significant skills on the part of the supplier.

3. **Routine:** this category represented non-strategic commodities and services where there were many alternatives to products or services, many sources of supply, a rather large number of low value, small individual items, and/or the component or service was generally considered a commodity.

4. **Leverage:** this category represented a strategic commodity where there would be significant expenditures, but where there was also large market capacity and capability. Additionally, there were significant opportunities for alternate suppliers and there was sensitivity to market and price pressures.

The next step was to analyze the role of suppliers being utilized to support the R&D function with respect to the overall commercial program. To do this, a new spreadsheet was developed to identify the various factors by which we wished to evaluate, and categorize, a supplier. The idea here was to establish a "criticality" factor and a "value-add" factor. The criticality factor was a qualitative assessment of how important a particular supplier was to the current R&D effort, whereas the value-add effort was a qualitative assessment by the commercial team regarding how much value the potential supplier could add toward meeting project demands in terms of price, schedule, and quality. Both factors were rated on a 0–1 scale with 0 being not critical and no value-add and 1 being extremely critical and very high potential for value-add. Exhibit 2-3 shows the determinants used and the specific categories by which criticality and value-add factors would be assigned. Exhibit 2-4 identifies the particular values for criticality and value-add factors. Exhibit 2-5 identifies the results for a particular supplier who supplied individual components for the downhole technology.

Once this exercise was completed for all suppliers identified on the bill of material (BOM) for the final product, the individual analyses were combined into a single executive summary as shown in Exhibit 2-6. Once we understood the level of criticality for a component or service and had gained some understanding into the nature of the supplier relationship that had been formed with the R&D team, we could then generate the next appropriate steps with regard to furthering the relationship. In our case, we had several suppliers that fell into the "critical" relationship category and, most importantly, both R&D and the commercial team understood the analysis and the reasoning behind the assessment.

As previously stated, this exercise was performed with all BOM items and services used to manufacture the final assembly. Once all materials and services relationships had been categorized, those relationships

Exhibit 2-3. Supplier Categorization Criteria

Specification complexity	Technology maturity	Process maturity	Service, equipment, or component	Market capacity (number of suppliers)	Supplier capability (technical capability and available capacity)
Critical–Conformance Required for Reliability and Performance	New technology–concept stages	New process–development stages	Service	<3 suppliers	Limited capability and limited capacity
Major–Conformance Required for Performance or Reliability, but not both	New technology–verification and validation	New process–verification and validation	Equipment	3–5 suppliers	Limited capability with adequate capacity
Minor–Conformance Does Not Impact Reliability or Performance	Existing technology	Existing process	Component	>5 suppliers	Adequate capability and limited capacity
					Adequate capability and capacity

Spend potential	Uniqueness of raw material	IP Risk and ownership	Patent protection	Purchase frequency	Level of development/ customization
>$1,000,000	Commodity–can easily be purchased on market, ample supply	IP owned by Firm, critical to Firm's competitive advantage	Patent exists–owned by Firm	Infrequent	Significant–requires both capital and R&D resources
$500,000–$1,000,000	Specialty–limited supply, limited qualified sources, potentially high demand	IP owned by supplier, critical to supplier's competitive advantage	Patent exists–owned by supplier	Frequent	Moderate–requires capital or R&D resources, but not both
<$500,000		IP not critical	Patent exists–owned by other		Limited–requires limited capital or R&D resources
			Patent does not exist–not needed		
			Patent does not exist–needed		

Exhibit 2-4. Definition of Criticality and Value-Add Factors

Response	Criticality	Value-add
$500,000–$1,000,000	0.50	0.50
<$500,000	0.25	0.25
<3 suppliers	0.90	0.90
>$1,000,000	0.85	0.85
>5 suppliers	0.20	0.20
3 to 5 suppliers	0.50	0.50
Adequate capability and capacity	0.40	0.70
Adequate capability and limited capacity	0.40	0.40
Commodity–can easily be purchased on market, ample supply	0.10	0.75
Component	0.00	0.00
Critical–conformance required for reliability and performance	0.88	0.78
Equipment	0.00	0.00
Existing process	0.20	0.70
Existing technology	0.45	0.75
Frequent	0.55	0.78
Infrequent	0.15	0.20
IP not critical	0.25	0.35
IP owned by firm, critical to firm's competitive advantage	0.90	0.85
IP owned by supplier, critical to supplier's competitive advantage	0.65	0.20
Limited–requires limited capital or R&D resources	0.25	0.25
Limited capability and limited capacity	0.70	0.20
Limited capability with adequate capacity	0.70	0.70
Major–conformance required for performance or reliability, but not both	0.50	0.50
Minor–conformance does not impact reliability or performance	0.15	0.15
Moderate–requires capital or R&D resources, but not both	0.50	0.65
New process–development stages	0.75	0.30
New process–verification and validation	0.75	0.45
New technology–concept stages	0.75	0.35
New technology–verification and validation	0.65	0.50
Patent does not exist–needed	0.85	0.65
Patent does not exist–not needed	0.15	0.15
Patent exists–owned by other	0.80	0.40
Patent exists–owned by Firm	0.80	0.80
Patent exists–owned by supplier	0.15	0.20
Service	0.00	0.00
Significant–requires both capital and R&D resources	0.90	0.75
Specialty–limited supply, limited qualified sources, potentially high demand	0.90	0.80

Exhibit 2-5. Supplier Relationship Evaluation

Supplier Name:			
Determinant	Criteria	Criticality score	Value-add score
Service, equipment, or component	Component	0	0
Technology maturity	New technology requiring verification and validation	0.65	0.5
Process maturity	New processes requiring verification and validation	0.75	0.45
Specification complexity	Critical conformance requirements required for reliability and performance	.88	0.78
Level of development/ customization	Limited thereby requiring capital and/or R&D resources	0.25	0.25
Spend potential	>$1M annual	0.85	0.85
Market capacity (# of suppliers)	<3 Suppliers	0.9	0.9
Supplier capability (technical capability and available capacity)	Adequate	0.4	0.7
Raw material uniqueness	Commodity material easily purchased	0.1	0.75
IP risk and ownership	IP owned by supplier and is critical to supplier's competitive advantage	0.65	0.2
Patent protection	Patent owned by supplier	0.15	0.2
Purchase frequency	Frequent	0.55	0.78
Average criticality score		0.56	
Average value-add score			0.58
Relationship classification	*Critical-Strategic technical*		

which fell into the "routine" and "leverage" categories simply followed existing firm contracting and procurement practices. For the "bottleneck" category, actions were taken to move these relationships into another category, and for those suppliers categorized as "critical," a combined team of R&D, commercial team, and firm supply chain members was established to start managing those relationships as the technology was further developed. This multi-disciplinary team then developed a series of standardized supplier engagement activities to further the firm–supplier relationship while meeting the needs of both R&D and the commercial

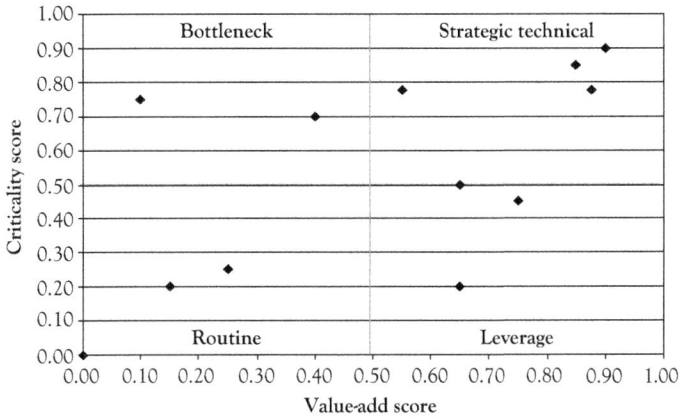

Exhibit 2-6. Relationship Determination

team. As new suppliers were considered, these evaluation practices were used to first determine the type of expected relationship with the potential supplier prior to financial commitments being executed.

Now you may be wondering something like, "Is this really necessary?" or "This seems to be a tremendous amount of work for something that should be obvious." Well, it was a lot of work, but the insights it yielded were tremendous and were later used in a war-game scenario (to be described in chapter 11). Just to keep the interest level up, the same supplier used in a war-game scenario, and the fact that the commercial team had categorized this supplier as a critical supplier did little to change the course of negotiations that occurred in the war game. For now, we will leave it to your imagination to think about how the various negotiation sessions were conducted.

Lastly, it is important to note that this was simply a qualitative assessment and was used as a screening activity to determine where to get started in managing the supplier relationships initially developed by the R&D group. It was not perfect, but it got us going in the right direction.

Having discussed the "buy" aspect of the "make versus buy" decision, how to identify existing relationships between the firm and its various suppliers, the framework we developed to identify which suppliers were of highest priority to us and why we needed to focus on them, let's now move to the "make" decision. In our particular case, we decided to elect a "make" decision regarding the final product assembly, based on the

Exhibit 2-1 analysis results. This brought on a whole new set of questions, and once again, we needed a direction to start heading in.

Supplier Landscape Analysis Results

As previously stated, we examined over 500 suppliers in North America, and none had the capability and capacity to meet our requirements; consequently, some sort of a manufacturing facility would be required. So while it is one thing to say we need a "plant", it is also a whole new scope of supply-chain development work since adding a plant to the supply chain is an exponential jump in supply-chain complexity. We now faced the following questions:

1. Where would the new plant be located?
2. What would be the scope of the plant?
3. Who would own and/or operate the plant?
4. What would be the cost of the plant, property, and equipment?
5. How does the plant align with the firm's core skills?
6. Is the plant really necessary?

The burden of proof was on the commercial development team to answer these questions (and many others!) to demonstrate that a plant was needed and to then define the scope of the plant. We decided to get out of the weeds for a little while and approach the issue from the proverbial 100,000 foot view. In essence, there were really only three choices to supplying the product. The first choice was that we could somehow and someway have suppliers supply everything to us. The other extreme was that everything was upon us. The third choice was to compromise between the two extremes. One may be thinking about now that the consideration of these three choices should be self-evident; however, at the time, it was not. The very idea of an oil and gas company starting a discrete manufacturing business unit to support exploration and production activities was extremely difficult to accommodate on the part of senior managers. After all, discrete manufacturing was not a core competency of the firm. This idea clashed with more than just a few paradigms, and the burden of proof fill to the commercial team to develop the best path for moving forward.

Supply Chain Concepts

Choice #1, which we will call the "virtual manufacturing plant," is identified in Exhibit 2-7.

In this particular supply-chain scenario, suppliers were responsible for every aspect of the supply chain up to, and including, final assembly of the product on-site at the project location. Referring to Exhibit 2-7, obviously there were more supplier relationships that existed; however, the key idea was that commodity suppliers would provide starting forms and/or components to intermediate processors. These intermediate processors would build sub-assemblies, which would then be shipped to a supplier performing the final assembly operation at which point the final product would be "sold" to the firm.

Choice #2, which we will call the "limited manufacturing plant," essentially places the firm in the place of the final assembly provider as shown in Exhibit 2-8.

There were two key differences between choice #1 and choice #2. The first was that the final assembly occurred at the deployment sites in choice #1, whereas the final assembly for choice #2 occurred in the limited manufacturing plant and the product was then shipped to the

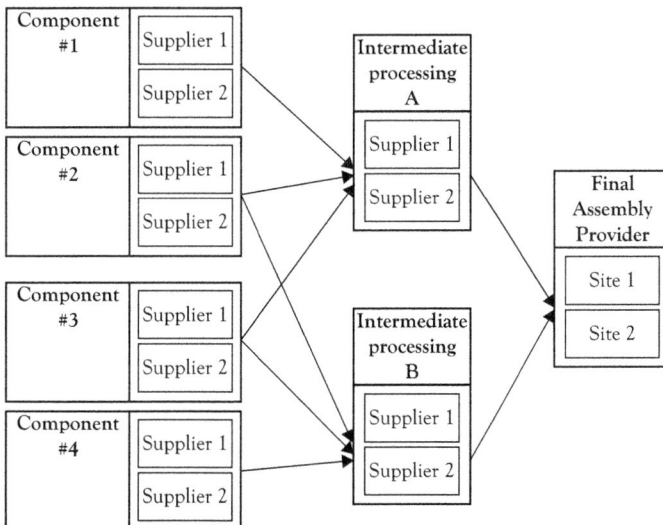

Exhibit 2-7. Supply Chain of the Virtual Manufacturing Plant

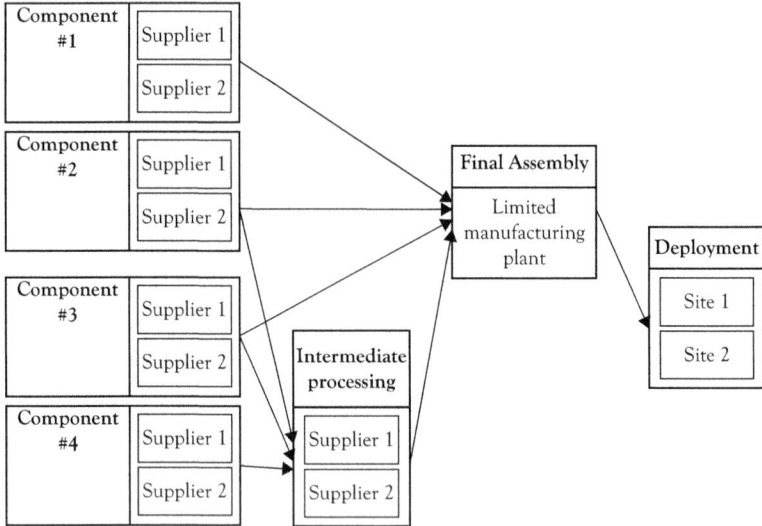

Exhibit 2-8. Supply Chain of the Limited Manufacturing Plant

deployment site. Custody of the final product occurred at the plants, which were located in close proximity to the deployment sites. The second key difference was that the limited manufacturing plant took on some intermediate processing steps and was limited in scope to only the technology presently being commercialized, that is, there was no provision to allow the scope of the plant to expand to future technologies under development by R&D. The idea here was that the plant would basically be a "throw away" as the expectation was that the technology development associated with the oil boom that was sure to occur, would drive competition between suppliers and the firm would no longer participate in discrete manufacturing.

Choice #3, which we will call a fully flexible and fully capable (FFC) manufacturing plant, is shown in Exhibit 2-9.

Starting materials, forms, and components would be brought into the FFC manufacturing plant, which was owned and operated by the firm. The firm was completely responsible for all manufacturing, intermediate processing, and final assembly activities inside the plant, and the finished product was then shipped to the deployment sites. Differing from Choice #2 in both scope and intent, provision was made in this plant to allow for

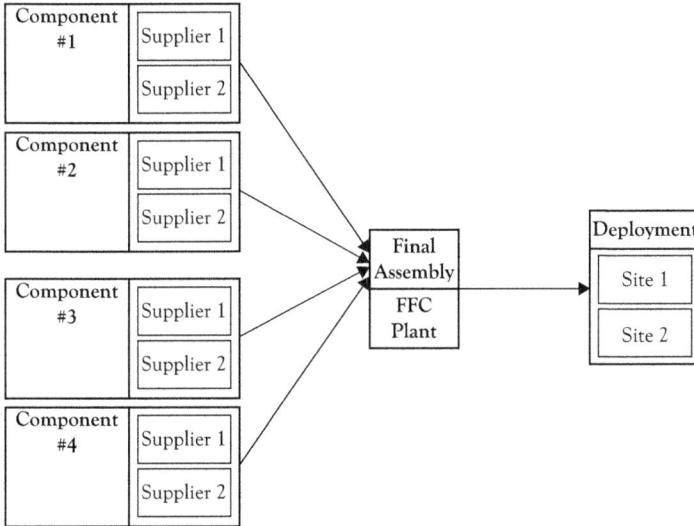

Exhibit 2-9. Supply Chain of the Flexible and Fully Capable Manufacturing Plant

production and technology expansions to accommodate future mass production of concepts that were actively being worked by R&D. So right now, one may be thinking perhaps that this is simply too obvious. It was, and it was not. While it is one thing to say, "get this from someone else, make part of it yourself, or go do it all by yourself," one needs to remember that there were severe intellectual property constraints and a completely inadequate supply base in terms of capability and capacity to support even the R&D effort in a timely fashion, much less a full-blown commercial project. We were inventing and performing design and technology changes daily, and our suppliers were simply not in a position to provide for us on anything more than a limited basis.

Having now defined three possible supply-chain scenarios, we wish to remind the reader that we were looking for a plausible and supportable supply-chain scenario that would meet project constraints with respect to timing, quality and costs. Precision and accuracy of cost and schedule estimates associated with any particular supply-chain choice would follow selection of the most plausible path in which senior management wished to proceed. We will now describe how we arrived to the most plausible and supportable choice that met the firm's requirements.

Qualitative and Quantitative Analyses

To determine the most attractive supply-chain scenario, we once again built a series of spreadsheets to allow us to compare and contrast these three choices over a period of several months. As a starting point, we attempted to perform some quantitative assessments by pitting choice #1 (which we will now refer to simply as the virtual plant) to choice #3 (which will be referred to simply as the flexible plant). An executive summary of this quantitative assessment result is shown in Exhibit 2-10.

Based on robust and extensive analysis, the commercial team determined that the virtual plant choice would be more expensive than the flexible plant choice in the range of $100M–$150M annually. In conjunction with the quantitative analysis, the team also performed a qualitative analysis on issues that were more difficult to measure. An executive summary of the qualitative analysis is shown in Exhibit 2-11. This analysis also concluded that the virtual plant was less advantageous to the firm with respect to the flexible plant. Simply put, the virtual plant exposed the firm to greater risk, in terms of product quality, erosion of intellectual property, accommodation of design changes, finance, and other considerations. The flexible plant was then compared to choice #2 (from now on simply called the limited plant). A similar analysis indicated that the flexible plant was superior to the limited plant.

Exhibit 2-10. Quantitative Estimate of Major Supply Chain Differences

Cost component	Virtual vs. flexible plant	Remarks
Quality and Performance Penalties	10%–20% Higher	Suppliers would still be required to make profits even when assessed performance penalties
Production Expense	10% Higher	Suppliers still required to maintain marketing, scheduling, production, and other administrative and overhead services as opposed to meeting needs of a single customer
Process Controls, Quality, and Production Scheduling Monitoring	2%–3% Higher	Required to have redundant personnel performing these functions across multiple facilities
Inventory and WIP	20% Higher	Based on a 10% holding cost rate
Raw Material Costs	3%–5% Higher	Suppliers most likely not have the same purchasing power as the firm

These quantitative and qualitative assessments took quite a bit of time to perform and included a significant work effort to set appropriate conditions for assumptions, boundary conditions, and so on. The end result was that we did demonstrate that the FFC manufacturing plant strategy was more advantageous to the firm than the virtual plant strategy and the limited plant strategy. Upon review and approval by senior management to proceed with the further development of the FFC manufacturing plant strategy, the commercial team then began a new series of work efforts to identify the scope of the plant, perform site selection analysis, transportation network analysis, and to develop high-quality cost estimates for both construction and operation costs. As it would be determined later, the total installed cost to the firm for the FFC manufacturing plant was ~$150M. Given the fact that the overall

Exhibit 2-11. Qualitative Assessment of Major Supply Chain Differences

Cost component	Virtual vs. flexible plant	Remarks
Transportation	Higher	Transportation scattered across many different facilities and many facilities would need to operate in series for intermediate processing
Learning Curve Capture	Lower	Little to no opportunity to capture learning curve benefits across a scattered supply base
IT Support	Higher	Little to no opportunity to capture synergies as suppliers have a variety of IT systems that would be difficult to integrate with the firm's systems
Accommodating Technology Changes	Higher	Multiple suppliers providing a broad spectrum of goods and services would find it difficult to accommodate firm design changes at the pace the design changes were expected to be produced
Intellectual Property Protection and Ownership	Very difficult	Firm expected many lawsuits closely related to the item above since it would become increasingly more difficult to properly attribute IP to either the firm or a supplier
Project Controls	Higher	The virtual plant must fit into existing supplier production runs. Firm unwillingness to provide scope of cost, quality, and schedule expectations to suppliers would simply drive prices up
Supplier Agreement Defaults	Could be many	Unless some critical suppliers had a fairly significant R&D function, firm technology changes could force suppliers to default on their agreements

multi-billion dollar project would have a life of 30–50 years, this was a bargain decision. Regarding the scope of the FFC manufacturing plant and how we demonstrated that the plant lowered our risk expectations for the entire project, these subjects are included in later chapters.

Do the Results Make Sense?

At this point, we want to back up just a bit and revisit the "make" decision with respect to manufacturing/fabrication versus final assembly. After all, what does "make" really mean? If one is buying components and assembling them into a final configuration, does that mean "make"? What if there are some things that are purchased in one form and in your process you change the form of the material to meet your requirements, does that constitute "make"? Within the make versus buy decision framework, does it even matter?

Just as the decision framework for make versus buy was applied to the product by breaking the product down into its six major sub-assemblies, the same framework was used to determine if leverage opportunities existed in any of the production processes used to manufacture each of the subassemblies. For example, in one instance, one technology required three different metals to be formed into a single metallic sub-assembly and we had only been able to identify two potential suppliers with sufficient capability and capacity to meet our R&D requirements. By using the decision framework with respect to the identified production processes, we were able to gain some very clear insight into the make versus buy issue and its implications in those particular supplier relationships.

As we re-examined each of the sub-assemblies from a process and mass production point of view, and by using the make versus buy criteria from Exhibit 2-1, we were more than just a little surprised to discover that nearly 80% of the sub-assemblies contained manufacturing process or production controls that we would need to exercise extreme control over to meet our quality control requirements. Additionally, there was significant manufacturing process control intellectual property being developed with our R&D suppliers and we were having extreme difficulty in negotiating appropriate contract language that protected both the firm and the supplier's interests. Since the firm would be required to be intimately involved with ~80% of all manufacturing and production processes associated with manufacturing sub-assemblies for the final product, in addition to having complete control over the production and assembly processes for the final assembly, it was simply easier to establish complete control over all elements with the facility owned and operated by the firm.

Now you would have thought that presenting the facts and the logic, this would have been a fairly straightforward argument to make and decision to take. We can tell you that it was not, and it was easily three years before the firm would accept these facts and make the commitment to move forward with an initiative to construct an FFC manufacturing plant that would produce and assemble the final product using starting forms and materials provided by commodity suppliers while allowing for future accommodation of new R&D technologies. This remark is not designed to disparage the firm in any way, it is included as a simple reminder that what ought to be self-evident and "easy" decisions are oftentimes far more difficult to execute given turbulent economic conditions, regulatory and legislative requirements, ever-changing project scopes, definitions, time-lines, and many other issues, which keep one's professional life interesting.

CHAPTER 3

Low-Cost Country Sourcing

The next level of argument that is generally encountered after "make versus buy" is the issue of why can't the work be done somewhere where the labor cost is lower than what it would be in the United States? This is a very fair question and to answer it one must now start also thinking about transportation costs, product/component quality, intellectual property protection, specific country rules and regulations, import duties and fees, and so on. These considerations are in addition to finding suppliers in another country with appropriate capacity and capability (as if finding them in the United States wasn't difficult enough!).

The low-cost country sourcing decision is not trivial, and if one thinks about the level of difficulty associated with taking a "make" decision, taking a "make" decision and then out-sourcing the making becomes even more problematic. That said, the "easy" part of the low-cost country sourcing decision was finding commodity suppliers capable of providing the plant with the appropriate quantity and quality of required material starting forms, bearing in mind that the risk of potential supply-chain disruptions could be greatly increased due to transportation, import/export legislation, customs duties and fees, social turmoil, volatile tariff and tax issues, inability to adequately protect intellectual property, and other issues/events outside of the control of the firm.

Getting Started

So how does one begin to determine if low-cost country sourcing would be an appropriate strategy for the firm to take on, considering that R&D for the final product may still be heavily in progress, design changes occurred daily, overall project scopes and timings are changing in response to global events, and so on? The first step is to determine high-quality cost estimates for manufacturing the final product, assuming that all of the technology improvements would be in place as of a given future date. The next step is to develop a path forward regarding how those costs would be reduced through further simplification of manufacturing process steps, increasing process speed, automation, material substitution, high volume material purchases, and so on. This analysis provides the first indication as to the initial commercial production costs for the final assembly. One also needs to understand the primary drivers behind all of the costs and associated cost reductions. The last step is to determine if there are any appropriate industry analogs by which one could compare expected cost structures to determine if there are any further opportunities for significant cost reduction. Once the cost structures and their associated drivers are understood, one is now ready to start addressing the issue of low-cost country sourcing.

In our particular case, as we considered various analogous products and associated manufacturing costs, it became evident that the benefit for low-cost country sourcing was limited. We were able to identify only a single opportunity that would provide a maximum of a 15% cost reduction on one subassembly, prior to consideration of any risks.

Details

To determine if this 15% opportunity was worth pursuing, we developed a risk matrix and criteria as shown in Exhibit 3-1, where LCC1 means Low-Cost Country 1.

The total risk score is the maximum point value obtained by multiplying the weight factor by the high risk value and then summing all of the criteria. Individual risk scores were determined by multiplying the risk assigned for each criterion by its associated weight factor and then summing all of the criteria. Low score wins. In this particular instance, we observed that if tariffs for a particular material returned to historical levels for Low-Cost Country 1, the 15% cost reduction we were anticipating would be immediately eliminated, and the product would actually incur a 5% cost increase. Given the price volatility associated with the materials that we were considering, we elected to not pursue low-cost country sourcing for this particular subassembly.

Exhibit 3-1. Weighted Qualitative Assessment for Low-Cost Country Sourcing

Determinant	Criteria	Low risk	High risk	Weight	LCC 1 individual score	LCC 1 weighted score
Political	Political instability	1	5	5	2	10
	Regulatory instability	1	5	3	2	6
Commercial	Loss of intellectual property	1	5	5	5	25
Technical	Lack of skilled labor base	1	5	3	3	9
	Lack of proper QA/QC	1	5	1	4	4
Operational/Organizational	Lack of Infrastructure	1	5	1	2	2
	Infrastructure instability	1	5	2	1	2
Paralyzing Disruptions	High frequency of natural disasters	1	5	2	1	2
	Lack of flexibility in handling supply chain fluctuations	1	5	3	5	15
Economic	Monetary instability	1	5	5	2	10
	High tariffs/fees/duties	1	5	3	4	12
	Maximum weighted risk score			165		
	LCC 1 total weighted risk score					97

Conclusion

In the end, we chose not to pursue low-cost country sourcing at all. The risks far outweighed the benefits, particularly at project start. Would this decision stay the same once the project became fully operational? Most likely not, however, since we did expect the final assembly technology to change significantly, there would be plenty of opportunities to re-perform this analysis.

CHAPTER 4

Intellectual Property

Intellectual property (IP) is a simple concept that seems to be extremely difficult to effectively implement. In its most basic form, the idea of IP says that one party cannot take credit for the ideas of another party. Practically speaking, effectively administering an IP policy that maintains the mutual trust and respect of each party is difficult to achieve. In the interest of taking a subject that some may not find particularly appealing, we will keep this chapter pretty concise.

Some Truisms

In the general case, there are some truisms regarding IP as follows:

- Most businesses find it necessary to have an IP strategy
- Third-party IP rights are usually not knowingly infringed upon
- IP-related agreements need to be properly executed
- IP disputes and related communications can consume tremendous resources
- Most IP agreements usually start out with what is the most advantageous to the parent company (of course).

IP can be one of the largest obstacles faced by R&D teams if they choose to involve a vendor from the supply chain to assist in solving a particular issue. What generally happens is that the R&D team will struggle internally for a period of time trying to resolve an issue and frequently, will resolve it with little to no outside assistance. But then comes a day when R&D is trying to push the boundary of currently well-known and well-established technology and now enters an IP issue for consideration and resolution PRIOR to involving a supplier. In our particular case, we desired to form a coil of tubing to take care of some transportation and delivery issues. In general, the process of coiled tubing formation is fairly straightforward as long as the wall thickness of the tubing is fairly thin, say 0.25 inches or less, and as long as the tubing is kept hollow. Well, we were working with extremely heavy walled tubing, far in excess of 0.25 inches, and we needed to have components inside the tubing. If that wasn't enough, the components inside the tubing were extremely brittle and would be required to withstand the bending forces during the coiling operation and straightening forces during the uncoiling operation. So we had two technology issues to deal with: the first issue was to progress currently available technology along for coiling and uncoiling of heavy wall tubing; and the second issue was to not break the stuff inside the tube during the coiling and uncoiling operations. Enter also two IP challenges.

The Typical Approach to IP

In our hurry to maintain project schedules, we engaged our leading suppliers having this coiled tubing technology to assist us in developing a viable solution to these issues. Now, one would think that the IP would be really straightforward with an approach being something like:

Firm: We will tell you, the supplier, what we want to do, but will not share any further information and we also do not want to know how you did it.

Supplier: We will find a solution for the two technology issues, but we get to do whatever we want with the found solution.

Seems pretty simple and straightforward, right? Nothing could be further from the truth. You see, the firm knew what they needed done and was smart enough to realize that soon the competition would follow suit. When that happened, this particular vendor would be pursued by the firm's competitors. The firm also had no particular desire to invest significant capital and resources in developing new manufacturing technology only to have it be essentially given away to competitors when they entered the marketplace. The suppliers also realized that the firm did not have a good understanding of the suppliers' customer base, and there was significant opportunity for them to market the technology with minimal investment in the technology development. After all, these suppliers were being compensated well to perform "one-off" production runs and various trials for the R&D effort. The suppliers also demonstrated their capability and capacity to learn at very rapid pace. Given the size and scope of the projects, and since the folks at the firm simply had a tendency to talk, in addition to developing the tradecraft and know-how for the new technology being developed, suppliers were <u>unwilling to cooperate</u> with the IP strategy of the firm and were simply not interested in having the firm exercise constraints over the use and marketing of the technology they assisted in developing.

Obviously, the trade craft and know-how belonging to each organization prior to their mutual engagement to solve an issue remained with the individual organization. The question was how to deal effectively and efficiently with knowledge that is developed as a result of the two parties working together. How does one account for their contribution? Unfortunately, there is not a "one-size-fits-all" answer; however, there is possibly a one-size-fits-all approach as shown in Exhibit 4-1 below.

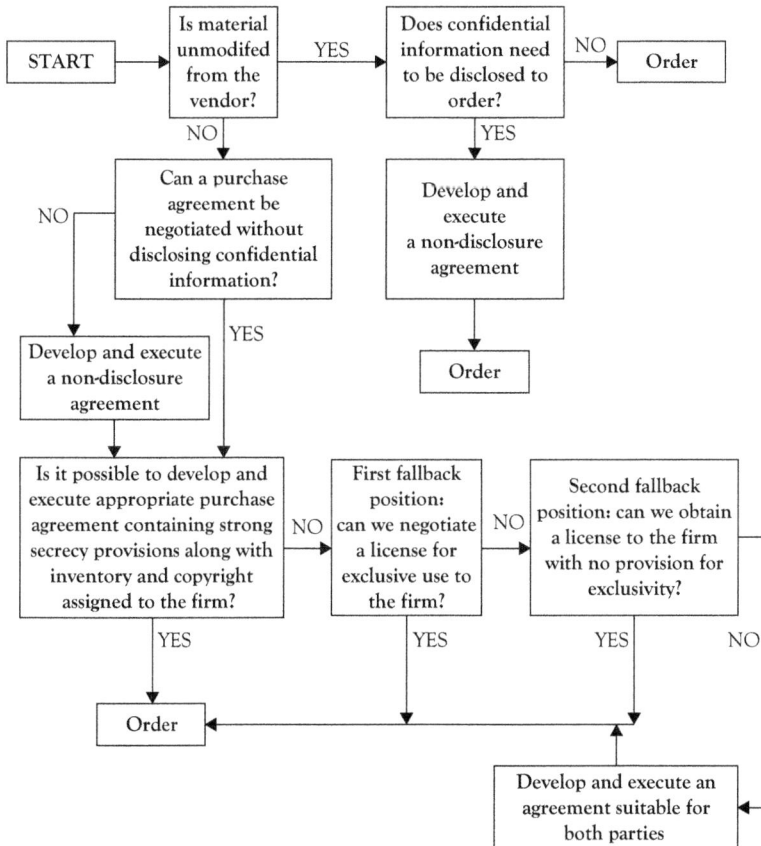

Exhibit 4-1. Flowchart for Intellectual Property Process

As promised, this chapter is concise, but please let us not underestimate its importance because of its brevity—after all, this is the sort of thing that keeps the "legal eagles" in business. As with anything else, a little bit of planning before the initial engagement with a supplier will go a long way toward keeping the IP issue manageable. Get involved with your supply chain and procurement professionals that are on staff. Figure out the things that need protection and those things that do not. Put together a simple, yet coherent, plan. Test drive the plan. Refine as required. Let us also not forget that suppliers who are reading this book may also be trying to achieve the same thing. Figure out what your drivers are. Don't try to control everything. Don't think that suppliers are going to cooperate simply because of your name or industry reputation. Always be gracious and respectful to suppliers, they know more about what they are doing than you do.

CHAPTER 5

Accommodating Design Changes

Accommodating design changes during new product development is a nightmare for commercial development managers, primarily due to the ripple effect design changes have on all other aspects of product development, but more importantly, due to the impact the changes have on suppliers. While design changes may be perfectly legitimate for improving product life, quality, function, reducing cost, and so on, a system needs to be in place to control the timing and manner by which design changes are incorporated into the base technology. While this may be a relatively simple statement and should be completely obvious, once again, in practical terms, it can be extremely difficult to implement. Contracts get negotiated for one design and then must be renegotiated for a second, third, and n^{th} design. Having a clear understanding of when and how design changes are expected to occur enables the development of strategies with suppliers in advance.

Stage-Gate Internal Alignment Issues

One of the most effective methods of accommodating design changes is to employ some sort of "stage-gate" process in the product design. A major issue of stage-gate processes can be one of achieving internal alignment within the process. We mean that, typically, the stage-gate process is developed around the major steps necessary to advance and complete the project on hand; however, the process usually does not account for linkages into the supply chain. For example, as our R&D folks continued to develop the product, one particular type of stainless steel was used in a primary component, and unfortunately, it had a somewhat constrained supply base. The next generation of the technology employed a different stainless steel, which was much more readily available. Returning to the "make" versus "buy" and supplier networking discussions, the size of the supply base for the new, yet untested material was a differentiator with respect to the type of relationship we thought that we would need to have with proposed suppliers.

So while the obvious answer was to integrate the stage-gate process of R&D with the firm's contracting and procurement process, in reality, this really only works well on paper. The reason for this is that the ratio of people in R&D to the people in supply chain is usually quite high therefore allowing little to no time for the supply-chain personnel to perform adequate due diligence. In our case, this ratio was about 80:1. What typically happened was a conversation such as this:

R&D: We need this product and it can be purchased from this particular supplier for this amount.

Supply chain: Who are the other suppliers?

R&D: Supplier 1, 2, and 3; however, Supplier 2 and 3 costs are higher, and they are unable to meet our requirements for a, b, and c.

Supply chain: OK, please fill out the appropriate requisition, and we will confirm that a contract is in place with this supplier. If not, we will have to set-up the new supplier in our database, which will take x days.

So with regard only to delivery price and schedule, a relationship with a supplier was established. Now then, this might be perfectly fine with regard to those supplier relationships, which are considered to be routine, but how would the supply-chain person ever know the importance of the relationship with respect to the commercial development of the product? One obvious answer was to embed the supply-chain person into the R&D group and to provide appropriate training with respect to relationship management. Adopting other tools such as "RACI" charts (for those unfamiliar with the term RACI–it stands for responsible, accountable, consult, inform; it was essentially a large spreadsheet with assigned roles for each of the team members) also helped smooth out the process; however, we were never able to really grasp the power of supply-chain relationship management primarily due to an organizational oversight—there were no performance metrics associated with annual business and personal performance goals. Everyone was measured differently, and since bonuses were tied to how well individual goals were accomplished, the internal alignment that needed to occur on this particular topic never matured.

Here is the point. If a firm is pursuing a path to utilize the supply chain as a serious competitive weapon in the marketplace, then all aspects of the firm–supplier relationship must be examined to determine where leverage points exist (if any) and how those points may be best utilized. The internal alignment between departments must be such that in common areas of supply-chain performance, such as supplier relationship management, appropriate business goals must be established to avoid sub-optimizing the business performance of the firm based on maximizing individual performance goals. There is obviously a balance that needs to be achieved between R&D and supply-chain goals and objectives, but at the end of the day, internal alignment must be achieved by the firm.

A Real-Life Example

We have digressed just a little bit here, so let's go back into the discussion. How do we best position both R&D and supply-chain personnel with regard to recognizing the type of relationship that needs to be established with new suppliers supporting changes in product technology? The following steps should help:

Step 1: Identify the dates for the first supplier support of technological changes that are anticipated.

Step 2: Utilize a spreadsheet and characterize the type of supplier relationship anticipated–perform the "make" versus "buy" analysis followed by the supplier networking analysis.

Step 3: Obtain consensus and alignment between R&D and supply-chain personnel regarding the *initial* status of the relationship.

Step 4: Execute the defined strategy for the relationship *slowly*.

Step 5: Revisit the relationship status after R&D has determined the probability of success for the anticipated technology change.

Why initial? Because one does not know how to proceed until the technology change is tested. Why slowly? Because one is trying to manage expectations. Let's explore this a bit more deeply.

As previously discussed, the project was all about identifying a novel method for hydrocarbon recovery from "difficult" oil reservoirs (i.e., hard-to-get-to-and-recover-without-going-broke-types-of-hydrocarbons!). The technology being developed was quite expensive, and thus the R&D group was deep into "hunting and gathering" information that would reduce costs and speed the development of the technology to recover the difficult oil. One day, some information became available regarding the potential use of ceramics in the technology, and an effort was launched to gather as much information on this particular application without giving away too much information on what it was that we were trying to accomplish. Sounds simple enough; however, it turned out that the supplier being considered was a "true blue" R&D firm and very disciplined with respect to how they engaged potential customers. From their point of view, they had a "customer engagement plan" that was well-thought out and well executed. They evaluated the potential impact of a new customer to their business, they had very robust intellectual property provisions in their contracts, and they did an excellent job of protecting their business drivers. While the firm represented "big oil" and had a preconceived notion that many suppliers would want to do business with them, it was quite shocking to learn that this particular supplier did not really think in these terms. It turned out that the firm's demands would represent only a small fraction of their business, and ultimately, the relationship did not fit their business model very well. So while interested in what it was that we were developing, their participation was really geared toward further developing and then selling the technology, the complete opposite of the firm's goals regarding intellectual property protection. The relationship did not end well.

Conclusion

Once again, the key to accommodating design changes successfully in the supply chain is to identify, as best and as early as possible, anticipated design changes and set forth an initial expectation and strategy as to how the supplier relationship will be defined and managed. Assuming that appropriate management attention has been directed toward achieving internal alignment between the R&D and supply-chain groups, and adopting some industry best practices toward relationship management, the results of the real-life example given could have been avoided. Consequently, the firm could have used the supply chain as a competitive weapon, instead of the supply chain becoming a source of problems.

CHAPTER 6

Learning Curves

Learning curves, also called experience curves, are closely related to accommodating design changes; however, the scope of learning curves is generally far broader. Learning curves take into account all aspects of the product, its operation, maintenance, processing, and essentially all cost elements that can be tied to the product. Some products experience learning curves on the order of 70%, whereas the learning curve for products associated with very mature industries can be far more modest at about 95%. The single biggest factor in accommodating learning curves in product development and project economics is developing an accurate model with clear boundaries, where a learning curve will start and stop with a given technology. For example, assuming that a 50% learning curve will be in place after five years may result in exemplary product and project economics, but are systems, processes and strategies in place to allow that learning curve to be captured? In our particular case, we wished to take a closer look at the following:

1. Was there an appropriate learning curve value that could be used in overall project economic analysis that would accommodate the migration from one specific technology to the next given the relative immature state of the starting technology?
2. Does each technology have its own learning curve or is a new learning curve generated for each technology improvement?
3. If a single learning curve can be developed, when should it start, and how would it best be accommodated in overall project economics?
4. Assuming technology changes occurred, how and when should these changes be incorporated, if sufficient time has not passed or the technology does not allow for root cause analysis to be performed for failures in the field?

5. If the organization chooses not to make the technology generally available to the marketplace, how should the "doubling concept" be considered if competitive market forces for the technology do not serve as incentives for cost reduction? (This one really hurt our heads!)

Background

Learning curves can be utilized, especially by materials-based manufacturers, to gain a view into how costs may be reduced over time. The learning curve has been in use by managers since the advent of modern management techniques. The idea behind the learning curve is simply that as the number of units produced increases, the associated unit costs decreases in an exponential and asymptotic fashion as shown in Exhibit 6-1. Some firms, for example, semiconductor and chemical firms, use learning curves to predict production cost of integrated circuits or batches of chemistries while utilizing the same production equipment. These same firms do not use their current learning curve to consider the impact of the insertion of new technologies, but rather, create new learning curves based on the realities of new production processes.

Usually it is a bit easier to view the learning curve as a straight line by using logarithmic functions as shown in Exhibit 6-2.

Important characteristics to note when assessing a product's learning curve are:

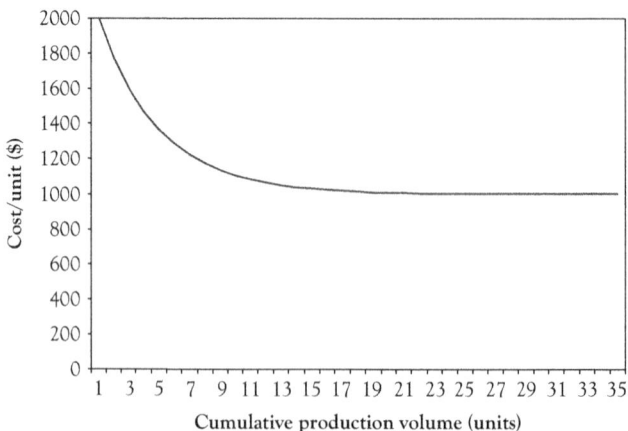

Exhibit 6-1. Conventional Learning Curve

Log (cost/unit)

○ ⌐Current cost¬

①
Initial cost estimate ➡ — ⬤ | Initial cost | ③
                                            Learning slope
                                            (learning rate)
                                            • Analogous process/situation
Log (y) = m*Log (x) + b   • Analogous product
where "m" = slope of the   • Analogous industry
learning curve

②
| Experience base |

Log (cumulative
production volume)

Starting volume to determine
number of doublings

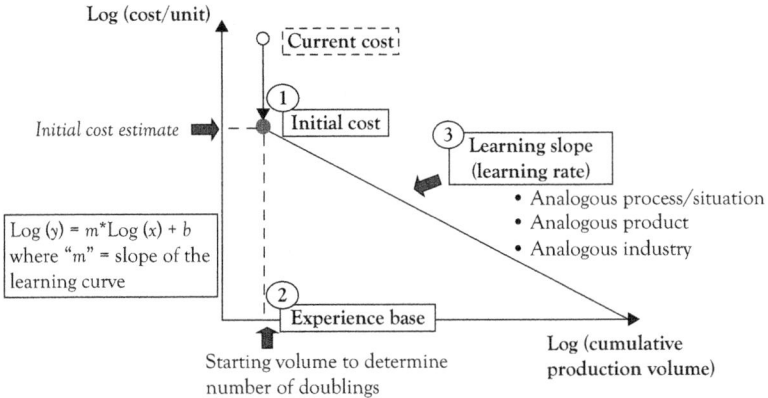

Exhibit 6-2. Learning Curve Using a Log Scale

(a) service or physical products;
(b) emerging or established technology;
(c) complexity of the product and/or manufacturing processes;
(d) number of subsystems in the product.

Complex products are characterized by:

(a) manufacturing processes with numerous and expensive capital equipment or extremely expensive building costs;
(b) highly skilled labor with many labor-intensive steps and that possess relatively low physical limits;
(c) processes with many subsystems requiring many steps or one system with many steps.

Non-complex products are characterized by:

(a) production processes with relatively few manufacturing steps and few costly pieces of equipment;
(b) elimination of much of the labor requirements through the use of automated and semi-automated systems;
(c) relatively high physical limits to the base costs;
(d) either having few subsystems or few steps in one system.

Large learning curve gains typically occur in materials-based products, which are characterized by high complexity and a high amount of labor. As a general rule, a product that has a cost basis of 75% machine operations and 25% direct labor offers much lower learning curve gains than a product that is characterized by 75% direct labor and 25% machine operations. Consider semi-conductor manufacturing. Ten to twenty separate and unique masking and metallization steps are used to manufacture most chips. The production process provides 100–400 unique opportunities to lower costs through learning curve capture. Most learning curve benefits are obtained through decreased labor costs, increased throughput, and increased yield.

The reasons that learning can occur as production experience accumulates, include:

(a) direct labor, indirect labor, and managers learn;

(b) specialization, standardization, and methods improve;

(c) small routine innovations drive incremental learning;

(d) capital learning – as production increases manufacturing equipment is more fully exploited, thereby lowering fully accounted unit costs;

(e) as a company acquires experience, it can alter its mix of inputs;

(f) as experience increases, minor design improvements are identified;

(g) suppliers and distributors also obtain learning curve benefits, thereby improving the supply chain;

(h) as product use increases, consumer use is more efficient and effective; spill-over effects suggest that efficiencies gained from one product can be applied to other similar products, between people and between organizations. The latter being especially true with information technology.

Examples of activities and associated learning curve rates are shown in Exhibit 6-3.

To accurately use learning curves for developing a better understanding of the cost of producing assembled goods, a company should make a significant effort to determine the learning curve effect on major product subsystems and the final assembled product. This information should then be used to create a cumulative learning curve. Finally, the insertion of new technology should be factored into the cumulative learning curve to produce an overall learning curve that not only combines incremental production-related improvements associated with the existing technology, but also accommodates insertion of new technologies. But where does

Exhibit 6-3. Examples of Industries and Associated Learning Curves

Product/industry	Time frame	Learning curve rate
Steelmaking	1920s–1950s	79%
Nuclear/Wind Energy	1990s	64%–79%
Repetitive Machining	1950s–1990s	90%–95%
Repetitive Electronics Manufacturing	1960s–1990s	90%–95%
Machine Tools	1960s–1990s	80%
Model T Automobile	1910–1926	85%

one start looking? Certainly Exhibit 6-3 can be used as a starting point, but it is also important to consider analogous situations and products in addition to analogous industries. Broadening the scope of learning curve capture into these three areas (analogous situations, products, and industries) will provide additional insight into opportunities to be considered for learning curve capture. The point is that it is probably fair to assume a 90–95% learning curve (meaning a five percent to ten percent reduction of costs associated with each doubling of production output) when preparing project economics, but determining if greater learning curve benefits can be captured will require significant time and management effort.

Application to Our Business

In our particular case, based on the production processes expected to be used for the starting technology, and equivalent (and also mature) production processes available in industry at the time that would be used to manufacture our technology, it became quite clear that we should expect no more than about a 5–10% reduction in costs over time due to learning curve contributions within the starting technology. The primary contributor to this situation was the fact that the bulk of material processes we would use were well established in industry and suppliers had little to offer for capturing learning curve benefits. Even when proposed design revisions were considered to the starting technology, it was quite clear that the project must accommodate significant technological changes to meet economic hurdles. In other words, we needed to leap from one technology to the next as soon as possible; however, the follow-on technologies were even more immature than the current technology.

The integration of major innovation is generally not considered a part of *conventional* learning curve theory. Typically, technology is integrated into an existing system if there is a belief that over time the product cost will decrease (and/or product value will increase). A diagram of two learning curves and one of the potential paths associated with the two learning curves is offered in Exhibit 6-4 for illustration. The top curve represents the initial learning curve believed to be in effect with the existing technology, and the bottom curve represents the new learning curve based on a significant change in product technology.

The danger here is that it is extremely easy to get trapped into thinking about what future costs are expected to be, accommodate these projections into present day project economics, and then taking a decision to move forward when the technology has not been adequately tested. So predicting cost reductions based on learning curve capture can be hazardous and the following health warning is hereby issued:

Health warning: Line of sight prediction of cost reductions is not always possible (i.e., defeats purpose of learning curves), but "people smoke in spite of health warnings."
People also speed in spite of speed limit signs—we think you get the idea.

In our particular case, if we assumed that all planned technology innovations were successful and that the most cost-favored technology

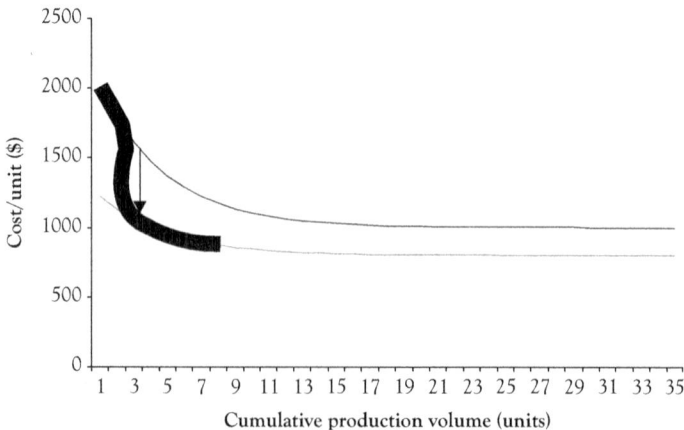

Exhibit 6-4. "Jumping" Across Learning Curves

and structure were used, our cost improvements had the potential to mimic an 85% learning curve.

Why then couldn't our particular technology obtain a more aggressive learning curve (e.g., 75%) in terms of per unit manufacturing cost? The short answer was lack of market forces. Simply because a particular technology is an innovative product, it does not follow that a high learning rate and associated learning curve capture will occur based on cumulative production. Once again, if we think back to the semiconductor industry, the first 25–30 years of semiconductor manufacture was dominated by captive users of semiconductors that integrated these products into other products that were then sold. Semiconductors were innovative and creative; production involved a number of highly skilled and labor-intensive operations, and an order of magnitude higher number of steps for completion compared to many other technologies. The market was also small. Over that 25- to 30-year period, market barriers to entry began to lower slowly, but it was not until the advent of the personal computer that significant market barriers dropped and demand skyrocketed. Since demand outstripped supply, learning curve capture tended to not be a high priority within manufacturing and production until the memory chip crash. In the late 1980s, there was a major oversupply of memory chips, plants were closed, jobs were lost, and competition became stiff because of market forces in play at the time. As a result, the cost of memory chips reached an order of magnitude lower than what it was 20 years before. In our case, the technology only offered 40 to 50 manufacturing steps to capture learning, not 400. We also had no intention of marketing the technology, which thereby significantly decreased the opportunities to reduce costs through production doublings.

Another issue to come to grips with respect to learning curves is that firms learn differentially over time and with respect to the physical limits associated to specific design, process, or technology. Some studies suggest that organizational learning, captured through savings in labor requirements, is greatest in the first three years after initial start-up. In contrast, capital learning extends over a much longer time period and appears to increase over time. This suggests that new entrants to the market are at a relative disadvantage on the basis of physical capital productivity. However, new entrants also appear to have a relative advantage in terms of organizational and labor learning, which occurs very rapidly. Some suggest that good entrepreneurs working with labor-intensive production techniques are able to learn faster and are therefore able to "out-compete" bureaucratic and formally managed incumbent firms as the learning effects attributable to the labor function are captured quickly.

Many consultants and practitioners also focus on predicting the "doubling" effect that can be obtained through the application of learning curves. However, this does not consider the asymptotic nature of learning curves over time. An easier way to consider the shape of the learning curve is to break a single nonlinear learning curve into two separate linear sections. The slopes of these two lines differ greatly and are determined by the forces that drive and retard learning curve benefits. The slope of the first line represents the early portion of a learning curve and is governed by the managerial capabilities, technological competency of a firm, and gains in the production of systems directly related to insights associated with initial movement from little knowledge of manufacture to great comfort with production requirements and opportunities. The slope of the second line is significantly smaller and is governed by the physical limits of the technology of choice. The first portion (or aggressive portion) of the curve is the portion of the curve associated with bringing the immature technology to a level mature enough to be deployed in the field. The second, or asymptotic portion of the curve, is defined by the technological limits of the system, processes, procedures and raw material costs.

In our particular case, a handful of possible technology changes were identified and subsequently integrated into project economies resulting in potential for savings through technology integration of approximately 50% of product cost. It was also anticipated that there would be additional savings associated with more effective and efficient manufacturing. That is, workers would require less time to complete tasks, scrap would be reduced, better organization of work areas, and other manufacturing improvements would occur. Ultimately, the savings associated with these costs would become limited solely by the base costs of the materials. To achieve lower costs for completed units, it became necessary to change the product technology, which required less raw material and raw materials that were less expensive. The change between product technology improvements would result in moving from a higher cost learning curve to a lower cost learning curve, would provide additional immediate savings, and would create a lower physical limit to the minimum possible cost. In Exhibit 6-5, learning curves for several of the new, yet extremely immature, technologies for the production of the same product are shown. As in Exhibit 6-4, each curve in Exhibit 6-5 represents what we believed to be the learning curve associated with that particular technology. The difficulty noted here is that the physical limit of the current technology's learning curve would never be reached, since a new technology would be introduced that would induce a new and lower learning curve. This situation would repeat itself as each new technology was introduced. In Exhibit 6-5 we illustrate the introduction of five new technologies and their corresponding learning curves, starting from the initial and current technology. While it is a "mistake" to view movement across the individual learning curves as a single learning curve, our view of this "mistake" was that it was an "academic splitting of hairs." We did not care about the source of the learning, we just wanted our costs reduced to the lowest practical level as quickly as possible. Our overarching strategy was to get the biggest bang for the buck out of each learning curve, by producing as few units as possible, thereby generating an overall learning curve that mimics the one shown in Exhibit 6-5. Keep in mind that Exhibit 6-5 represents a fairly idealistic approach. The reality was that we were constrained by funding, manpower, and the duration of field trials which would cause these learning curves to be more staggered in their starting points with respect to time.

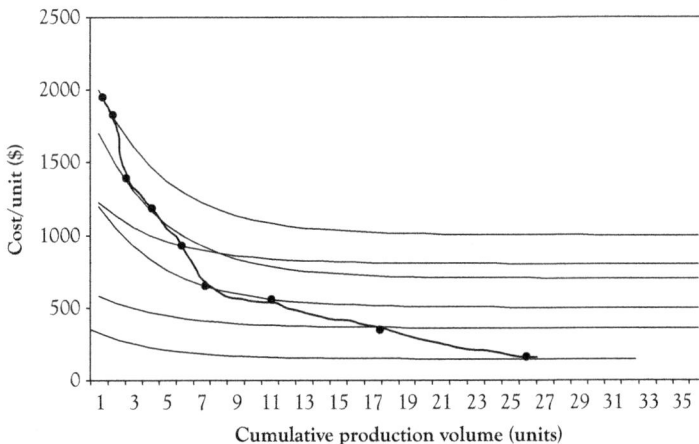

Exhibit 6-5. Combining Learning and Technology Integration and Generating a Single Learning Curve

Another question posed was when to start including or counting learning curve effects. For mass produced products, counting typically starts at the time that volume manufacturing is launched. In our case, we were extremely interested in the learning curve cost reductions that would occur prior to any significant capital equipment being purchased. We chose to use the actual costs of the first prototype that passed all field trials as the start of the learning curve for that particular technology.

One last idea to consider regarding learning curve capture is to approach learning curves from a systems perspective. It must be realized that systems learning occurs over longer period of time and that this learning usually starts at a later time compared to the curve for the initial technology. To make a cookie baking analogy, just because you have Grandma's cookie recipe does not mean that the cookies you make taste like Grandma's the first time out of the oven. The equipment and ingredients may be the same, but Grandma simply has more learning in her "cookie making system" than what the recipe identifies.

It is also necessary to gain operational experience to establish the start of the learning curve for the entire system. Learning curves are governed by the opportunity to learn, individually at first, and then as a whole, and are a function of the mechanisms chosen to accomplish the work processes. Given the maturity of the starting technology and its follow-on technologies, the lack of market forces, and the high-cost of raw materials, it was wrong, and naive, to arrive at the conclusion that after a given number of production units (256 in our case), the production cost would be about 10% of the original, if one believed that a 75% curve was truly achievable. Remember the health warning? Line of sight prediction on cost reduction can be hazardous to your health.

Realizations

Given the above discussion, one should realize the following before expending a tremendous amount of effort in accommodating learning curves in project economics:

1. While learning curves have been highly successful at estimating changes in labor productivity that occur after the onset of production

operations, the technique is less suitable for considering overall cost—unless cost and labor productivity are highly correlated.

2. If substantial effort is devoted to preproduction engineering and planning resulting in higher than normal labor productivity, the rate of learning will be lower.

3. Learning rates vary substantially among industries, products, and types of work. Past learning rates are guides, not rules or laws. Consequently, an overreliance on publicly stated learning rates is risky.

4. The rate of learning is time dependent and progress does not continue indefinitely. Asymptotes will be reached as the physical limits of material, processes, and equipment are reached.

In our case, and unlike semiconductors that start with low-yield/high-defect rates, it was anticipated that scrap and defect rates for our products and associated components would be very low, therefore learning curve benefits would be limited most likely to reduction of scrap, time, labor, inventory, set-up costs, energy, and other process-related events involved strictly in production. Unlike aircraft, ships, and vehicles, there was a relatively small number of parts, so there were fewer opportunities for learning curve gains. As much of the cost associated with the technology was directly related to base material costs, the physical limits to cost reductions through learning were limited to be somewhere between 70% and 90% of the cost of the product.

So where are we at? Cost reduction through the "learning by doing" approach is comprised primarily of reducing cost through labor productivity, minor innovations, lower capital costs, organizational learning, energy efficiency, and other incremental volume-related savings. Cost reduction accomplished by technological advancements is equivalent to jumping across individual product learning curves. This approach focuses on improvement by adopting new learning curves with strategically directed organizational learning and technology development and then by integrating volume-based learning in the more traditional fashion of learning by doing. Strategically directed learning can be accomplished within a given technology and structure through technology innovation and integration only if mechanisms are in place to force the jumps across the learning curves. The central difference between movement among design revisions within a technology and movement among different technology improvements is that movement among different technology improvements can result in a substantial reduction in the physical limits of the learning curve.

So here are a few guidelines in taking on the learning curve question. Greater opportunities for learning curve capture occur when:

1. There is high complexity of products and processes
2. There are high labor requirements
3. Firms are interested in learning and in taking a strategic approach that forces learning.

Returning to the R&D Discussion

You may be wondering at this point how all this discussion relates back to supply chains and research and development. First, it is important to understand that decreases in supplier costs are not automatically given to the buyer. As a matter of fact most suppliers seek to retain as much of the cost benefit as they possibly can. One's knowledge of learning curves, and where a particular supplier is at with respect to capturing learning curve gains is necessary to develop effective supplier engagement strategies.

Second, the application of the learning curve concept, and potentially using it to reduce costs, does not seem to be a realistic approach when dealing with commodity suppliers, but may work well with those suppliers that would be considered as "captive" to your requirements. If a captive supplier's books are open to the customer as a whole, then the customer can identify and hopefully extract learning curve benefits. The difficulty with this approach is that firms that operate on a cost-plus basis are not motivated to find learning curve benefits. In fact, if profits are negotiated as a certain percentage of costs, it is advantageous for the supplier to try and inflate costs to ensure the highest possible profit.

Third, inducing internal and external competition through consideration of make versus buy decisions may change the entire thought process on supplier relationships. In the research and development phase, significant emphasis must be placed on the make versus buy analysis.

If potential suppliers are almost as disadvantaged as you are with respect to your product requirements, there is significant opportunity for the firm to capture the learning curve all to themselves by taking a "make" decision as opposed to a "buy" decision for the particular product. Of course, one should also expect some upper management arguments along the lines of "manufacturing this widget is not our core competency" and/or "why can't we just pay someone else to do it?" In our case, we were simply unable to present a business case to different suppliers that provided sufficient motivation in terms of project timing, product costs, change orders, risk management, and so on, to effectively engage suppliers to share learning curve benefits as part of our research and development program. We paid top dollar on non-commodity items mostly because we were an interruption to our suppliers' production processes. Additionally, when our suppliers considered the future potential of their participation in our technology development and project scopes, their more pressing needs of today far outweighed the opportunities of the future. As one supplier said, "hope is a great breakfast but a lousy dinner."

Final Thoughts

Hopefully by now, a few ideas regarding learning curves and their impact to the supplier engagement strategy are beginning to form. Of equal importance is that one must also understand the reluctance on the part of suppliers to participate in learning curve benefits as part of the overall supplier engagement strategy. Additionally, there should be a couple of ideas regarding how to fend off management intent on using learning curves to make project economics look better and why doubling does not automatically reduce costs. Oh, by the way, in case you were wondering what we ended up doing, we used an overall 85% learning curve in our economics. This was based on an 82% learning curve with the starting technology which then moved to a much cheaper alternative that was 3–4 years behind in development but which only had the potential for a 95% learning curve. Since we were not planning on marketing the technology, we eliminated the opportunity for market forces to drive down costs through competition. Ultimately, we abandoned the effort to try and establish a "system" learning curve. Our 85% curve was strategically directed and jumped from one technology to the next. It also assumed that any field failures associated with each of the new technologies under development would quickly resolve themselves to meet commercial project requirements. Perhaps it was a bit conservative, but we must remind you of the previously stated health warning:

> *Line of sight prediction of cost reductions is not always possible (i.e., defeats purpose of learning curves), but "people smoke in spite of health warnings."*

CHAPTER 7

Risk as a Measure of Total Cost of Ownership

So the product specifications have not been solidified, design changes are still occurring, and the boss wants to know, "How do I show that the supply-chain strategy that has been developed is the lowest cost strategy and results in the lowest total cost of ownership for the product?" Wow! No problem, right? Perhaps we should try answering this question by performing some qualitative assessments with regard to risk.

What is risk? Dictionary definitions include "effect of uncertainty on objectives," "someone or something that creates or suggests a hazard," and "a factor, thing, element, or course involving uncertain danger: a hazard." More importantly, how are risks mitigated? Through insurance. So the principle here is one that suggests that if we have an idea of what constitutes significant risks, then the following question should be addressed: what types and kinds of "insurance" policies can be established to protect the firm from these risks?

The chapters on cost modeling and "make" versus "buy" provide glimpses into some risk factors that we considered, but here, we wish to be more replete with respect to the analysis performed regarding the supply-chain strategy of building our own manufacturing plant to deliver the product. Let's proceed directly into this example.

Risk Defined and Categorized

First, we categorized our risks starting at a very high level. This is important as it sets the direction for follow-on analyses. After defining several categories, we then divided them into sub-areas and definitions as shown in the following six exhibits.

Exhibit 7-1. General Category–Technical Risks

Sub-area	"Low" risk (1)	"High" risk (5)
Existing Supply Chain Capability	Capability currently exists	Capability is non-existent
Existing Supply Chain Capacity	Capacity currently exists	Capacity is non-existent
Intellectual Property Protection	Little leak potential	High leak potential
Manufacturing Quality Control	Largely internally controlled	Largely externally controlled
Manufacturing Control Points	Few control points	Many control points
Manufacturing Synchronization	Easy to synchronize with supply chain	Difficult to synchronize with supply chain
Production Schedule Optimization	Able to optimize centrally	Unable to optimize across supply chain
Supply Chain Stage Expertise	High expertise at each stage of supply chain	Limited expertise at each stage of supply chain
Climate	Temperate	Arctic

Exhibit 7-2. General Category–Economic Risks

Sub-area	"Low" risk (1)	"High" risk (5)
Direct Supply Chain Cost Influence	Large operational influence over supply chain costs	Limited operational influence over supply chain costs
Learning Curve Capture	Supply chain captures all learning curve benefits	Supply chain captures no learning curve benefits
Production Schedule Complexity	Realistic and risked	Aggressive and un-risked
Relative Risk of Vertical Market Failure	Demand easily met with alternative suppliers	Probability of supply equaling demand is low and few alternatives exist
Outbound Transportation	Load sizes and distance minimized	Heavy loads moving long distances
Learning Curve Generation	Scenario develops steepest learning curve slope	Scenario has minimal learning curve slope potential
Inbound Transportation	Load sizes and distance minimized	Heavy loads moving long distances
Relative Capital Expenditure Risk	Limited capital expenditures at supplier locations	Many capital expenditures at supplier locations

Exhibit 7-3. General Category–Commercial Risks

Sub-area	"Low" risk (1)	"High" risk (5)
Labor Availability	Sufficient labor pool	Limited labor pool
Relative Reliability Risk	Schedule adherence can be met	Schedule adherence difficult to meet
Network Complexity	Few supply chain nodes and simple interfaces	Many supply chain nodes and complex interfaces
Supplier Power	Use great deal of supplier capacity representing significant supplier revenue	Use little supplier capacity and represent small supplier revenue
Existing local labor content	Little dependence	High dependence
Contractual Interfaces	Single contractor	Many contractors
Supplier Dependence	Large portfolio of suppliers exist	Single suppliers
Relative Risk Ownership	Contractually clear and appropriate	Unclear and inappropriate
Contractor Competition	Commodity sourcing	Few competitors (i.e., <5)

Exhibit 7-4. General Category–Organizational Risks

Sub-area	"Low" risk (1)	"High" risk (5)
Number of Corporate Cultures	Single culture	Many cultures
IT Implementation Risk	Limited changes to existing IT infrastructures needed	Major changes needed to large number of IT systems needed
Number of Execution Locations	Single	Multiple (i.e., >3)
Control Points	One per echelon	Multiple points per echelon

Exhibit 7-5. Category–Political Risks

Sub-area	"Low" risk (1)	"High" risk (5)
Non-governmental Organizations/ Environmental Risks	No issues	Many issues
Supplier Network Complexity	Limited network	Complex network
Supplier Network Involvement	Passive	Active/Obstructive
Industrial Relations	Good	Militant
Manufacturing Legacy	Many manufacturing industries present	Many non-manufacturing related industries

Exhibit 7-6. General Category–Supply Chain Paralyzing Disruptions

Sub-area	"Low" risk (1)	"High" risk (5)
Labor-Related Shutdowns	No labor issues	Labor stoppage at single location
Product Quality Related Shutdowns	Few quality-related issues	Many quality-related issues
Product Reliability Related Shutdowns	Product life cycle and expectations are met	Product reliability-related failures cause significant supply chain disruptions
Single Plant Shutdown	Supply chain can continue with little interruption to product deliveries	Supply chain halted completely
Capacity Shortages	None	Single location presents greatest capacity shortage

Performing Qualitative Assessments

The second step was to assign weighting factors to each of the sub-areas and to work out any differences with regard to the assigned weight of the individual risk elements. The third step was to evaluate and assign a score to each risk topic with respect to the three overall supply-chain strategies (virtual manufacturing plant, from now on called virtual; limited manufacturing plant, from now on called limited; flexible and fully capable manufacturing plant, from now on called flexible). If you recall from Chapter 2, these three supply-chain strategies were pitted against each other, in a qualitative manner and at a very high level, to obtain an overall risk score for each strategy. The overall risk score is calculated by multiplying the individual category score by the weight of the category and then summing for each strategy. Lowest score wins. See Exhibit 7-7 for final results of this in-depth risk analysis.

Last but not least, it was very important to check the analysis for bias and determine if and where biases were occurring. It is a fair challenge to the team performing the analysis that, to put it bluntly, "you are not cooking the books." While everyone would agree that the "books were not cooked" because of the time investment, the excruciating challenge of going back and forth between the technical experts in the sessions, and the level of detailed analysis performed, it was simply easier to eliminate the challenge up-front by performing some bias analysis and answering the challenge before it was asked.

Exhibit 7-7. Comparison of Three Supply Chain Strategies (from Chapter 2)

Risk sub-area	Weight	Virtual	Limited	Flexible
Existing Supply Chain Capability	5	2	2	2
Existing Supply Chain Capacity	5	4	4	5
Intellectual Property Protection	5	5	4	3
Manufacturing Quality Control	4	5	4	2
Manufacturing Control Points	4	4	3	2
Manufacturing Synchronization	3	5	4	3
Production Schedule Optimization	3	5	4	2
Supply Chain Stage Expertise	2	4	3	2
Climate	2	3	4	4
Direct Supply Chain Cost Influence	5	5	4	3
Learning Curve Capture	5	4	3	1
Production Schedule Complexity	4	5	4	3
Relative Risk of Vertical Market Failure	3	4	3	2
Outbound Transportation	3	4	3	2
Learning Curve Generation	3	3	2	1
Inbound Transportation	2	1	2	3
Relative Capital Expenditure Risk	2	4	3	3
Labor Availability	5	1	3	3
Relative Reliability Risk	5	4	5	4
Network Complexity	5	4	3	2
Supplier Power	4	5	4	3
Existing local labor content	4	1	3	3
Contractual Interfaces	3	5	4	2
Supplier Dependence	3	2	3	4
Relative Risk Ownership	2	5	3	1
Contractor Competition	1	2	3	4
Number of Corporate Cultures	4	5	4	2
IT Implementation Risk	3	5	4	3
Number of Execution Locations	2	4	3	2
Control Points	2	4	4	2
Non-governmental Organizations/ER	5	2	3	3
Supplier Network Complexity	4	5	4	3
Supplier Network Involvement	3	5	5	4

(Continued)

Exhibit 7-7. Comparison of Three Supply Chain Strategies (from Chapter 2) (Continued)

Industrial Relations	3	2	3	3
Manufacturing Legacy	3	1	2	2
Labor-Related Shutdowns	5	3	5	5
Product Quality-Related Shutdowns	5	3	5	5
Product Reliability-Related Shutdowns	5	4	4	4
Single Plant Shutdown	4	3	5	5
Capacity Shortages	3	3	5	5
Overall Risk Score	715	521	522	429

Final Thoughts

This method of qualitative analysis provided some fairly interesting insights. Of particular interest was "why" the "limited plant" strategy was essentially no different than the "virtual plant" strategy. The answer was contained in the very name of the strategy "limited plant." Since this strategy did not accommodate the next generations of product technology, and performed few other roles outside of final assembly; as the next generations of product technology were developed, the "limited plant" would not fit (it was, after all, a "throw away" plant). At the same time, the "virtual plant" would require nearly a total redesign as the product technology changed, and newer, less expensive, and more robust products were developed out of R&D.

By coupling this qualitative analysis with the analyses performed in Chapter 2, we were able to develop an overall answer to the question presented toward the beginning of this chapter: "How does one show that a chosen supply-chain strategy is the lowest cost strategy and results in the lowest total cost of ownership for the product?" We simply argue, from both qualitative and quantitative positions, that the strategy with the overall lowest risk ensures the lowest overall total cost of ownership. If one wants to know by "how much" the strategies differ, one must now turn to the chapters on decision framing and cost modeling.

So how does this type of analysis help the discussion of R&D and supply-chain development? Quite simply, the analysis establishes direction. It is now easier to define the roles and responsibilities of the suppliers participating in the supply chain since the team has developed a high-level strategy to pursue. Initial analyses on "make" versus "buy," "low-cost country sourcing," "intellectual property," and so on, can be revisited to determine if any differences need to be accounted for in light of the overall strategy and appropriate tactics and action plans developed to address these differences. "Talking points" for the various team members can also be developed to address supplier questions and greatly assist in managing supplier expectations and overall firm–supplier relationships.

CHAPTER 8

Cost Modeling

Every product has a cost structure, and good cost models are imperative for being able to understand complex business situations. But what happens when the product is simply "too complex"? There are "too many" processing points, "too many" uncertainties, and "too many" risks? This chapter will explore a couple of different approaches to developing cost models and then demonstrate how using those models assists in supplier engagement strategy development.

High-Level Risk Model

The first model to discuss is what we called a "high-level" risk model (HLRM). This model was designed to assist the project team in gaining insight regarding possible hedging strategies and their associated costs, against catastrophic events at various supplier locations, which would cause random disruptions of random durations to the overall supply chain. This model was built using a sophisticated spreadsheet with ability to accommodate various probability distribution functions.

Examining the proposed supply chain from a high level, and recognizing that we were dealing with a constant demand for the product, we were interested in the following questions:

1. If the deployment of the final product was a random variable, but its demand was constant, what would be the impact on the supply chain of such deployment randomness? In other words, if the end-user had a tendency to "under-consume" the product on some days but "over-consume" the product on other days, what must be done with the supply chain to deal with these sorts of statistical fluctuations?
2. If the time between catastrophic events is random, and the duration of catastrophic events is random, what is the impact on the supply chain of these events?

3. What would be the magnitude of holding costs if the product was available but not deployed and the impact on opportunity costs if the product was not available when required?
4. Ultimately, how large of a buffer stock of finished product would be required given the questions above?

Developing an Analogy

To begin building a model, we took a step back and examined a real-world situation: a newspaper vendor who has to decide the number of newspapers to have at the beginning of each day. Newspapers not sold at the end of the day represent a loss; an insufficient number of newspapers leads to a forgone profit (an opportunity cost). Using the newspaper vendor problem as a framework, we developed the HLRM to provide insight into questions 1 to 4 above.

The HLRM assumed the following:

1. Product deployment could be modeled as a Poisson random variable.
2. The frequency and duration of catastrophic events could be modeled using exponential random variables.
3. Final assembly of the finished product had a random capacity which could be modeled using an exponential random variable.
4. Catastrophic events only occurred in the final assembly process; thereby the hedge would be a buffer stock of finished products.
5. If the final product was available but not needed, an inventory holding cost would be incurred. If the final product was needed but not available, a non-deployment opportunity cost would be incurred.

The major HLRM output was a graph that essentially identified the optimal number of finished products to carry as a buffer stock. Fewer products would result in lower service levels and higher opportunity costs. Additional units would result in higher service levels but also higher inventory holding costs. Exhibit 8-1 provides an example of the HLRM output.

We do realize that a huge leap was made in the last couple of paragraphs and one may be thinking, "This is totally unhelpful." The point here is

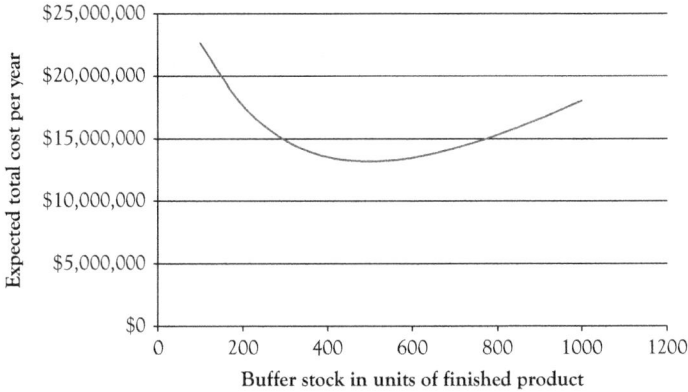

Exhibit 8-1. Example of the HLRM Output

not necessarily how the model worked, but understanding and generating further, deeper, questions to ask, and hopefully answer with the next-generation model. We simply wanted some insight into how much of a buffer stock would be required as insurance against various uncertainties and risks. Examining Exhibit 8-1, one observes that the optimal number of finished products to carry was approximately 500. Fewer than 500, we would experience a rise in non-deployment opportunity costs. More than 500, we would see a rise in inventory holding costs.

Now then, one may also be wondering why we would ever look at this in this way and what in the world does this have to do with R&D. The point was that R&D personnel did not have a view into the commercial aspects of the project, and while they were under a mandate to "reduce costs" for the product (and which R&D organization has never heard this?), it was important to prioritize cost-reduction initiatives. If one were to ask R&D how many finished goods needed to be carried in stock at any given time, there was simply no methodology in place to answer the question. From their viewpoint, the answer would be "zero" and the commercial folks should be pursuing a "just-in-time" supply-chain strategy. However, from the commercial viewpoint, failure to deliver finished goods resulted in non-deployment opportunity costs. That is, lowest cost does not result from lowest inventory. While one would never find non-deployment opportunity costs on a balance sheet, the end result of not being able to install and commission the final product would be increased project costs, delayed production, and ultimately, being late to market with hydrocarbons. A buffer stock of finished products could be justified, and it was important enough to do more than just "guesstimate" the appropriate quantity. After all, millions of dollars were at stake.

An additional point also needs to be made, that being, management did not have a clear view into the impact of how random consumption would impact the overall supply chain. While it was generally recognized that buffers would be required for various aspects of the project, gaining insight into the magnitude of expected buffer costs associated with this particular product was enlightening. Given the limited supply-chain base that we were experiencing, having a view into the number of finished goods that we would require to be carried as a buffer stock simply translated into how big of a warehouse would be required, where would it be, who was responsible, and so on—the easier questions to answer.

As with any good model, the HLRM simply generated more questions than it could answer, which brings us to the next generation of model that we called the business allocation model (BAM). In this model, we attempted to answer the question of "if we had only three suppliers for each of our major components and subassemblies of the finished product, how would we go about allocating our business among them given that each had different capabilities, capacities, locations, and costs?"

Business Allocation Model

To get started, we revisited the newspaper vendor analogy and attempted to use it at each step of the manufacturing process of the final product. Of course, the analogy did not fit well in all cases, but based on the experience of the HLRM development, we were a bit more prepared. The BAM was designed to identify the appropriate allocation of key components amongst suppliers based on price, location, normal business variation, and paralyzing disruptions/catastrophic events. Unlike traditional supply-chain deterministic optimization, this model incorporated different levels of uncertainty originating at supplier locations and used these uncertainties to determine nominal capacity and service levels, and ultimately, the impact on our demand for the complete assembly. In other words, since we were expecting to have a constant demand of the final product, how would supplier interruptions affect that demand and what would we then do to mitigate supply-side risks? In conjunction with the HLRM previously developed (as a reminder the HLRM only considered catastrophic events during the final assembly/production processes), how would accommodating buffers at each of the supplier locations serve to mitigate risks associated with supply-chain disruptions incurred in final assembly? There are fairly efficient methods to solve large-scale stochastic problems like the one we were facing, such as Bender's decomposition or the sample average approximation (SAA); however, we wanted to develop a simple heuristic model that could easily be manipulated via a spreadsheet. The issue that we faced was that our simple heuristic model ended up being not that simple, and it had to be eventually decomposed from an initial nonlinear programming problem formulation into two "easy-to-solve" linear programming problem formulations, where the solution from the first problem was used as the input to the second problem. This heuristic also took advantage of the flexibility of various spreadsheet functionalities to optimize average functions, in addition to the added cost benefit of not being required to purchase more sophisticated optimization software along with associated training, IT support, and so on.

Defining Uncertainties

Getting started, we wanted to have a view into supplier random variation. Given that supplier capacities were subject to random fluctuations due to normal business variability, it was important to try and account for random disruptions inherent to the supplier's operations (machine breakdowns, strikes, maintenance, etc.) and paralyzing disruptions caused by unexpected catastrophic events such as snowstorms, floods, earthquakes, acts of God, and so on. One might think that we were being just a bit overly ambitious with respect to trying to model things of this nature, and you might be right; however, given the constant demand nature of our product, it was absolutely imperative that we mitigate as much risk as possible on the supply side.

Because of the presence of uncertainty at each supply stage, the objective of this model was to define the best diversification and safety stock level allocated to each supplier, which would then minimize the total expected supply-chain cost. This model also accommodated utilizing Monte Carlo simulation approach for scenario generation to determine overall optimization and diversification among three suppliers for each of the major subassemblies. The scenario generation and heuristic optimization procedures were implemented in a spreadsheet via a user's interface. The main result of this development was the analysis of the impact of diversification in strategic sourcing decisions, under the presence of stochastic supply disruptions.

As stated, we assumed a two-stage supply-chain network with a single finished product. This finished product was formed from six different subassemblies consisting of several key components. Most of the components for these subassemblies were commodity-type items so typical supply-chain practices associated with commodity purchases were assumed. Each subassembly was then assembled into a single product in a final assembly operation. The bill of materials (BOM) structure is 1:1 for each subassembly in relation to the final product. See Exhibit 8-2.

Additionally, each component of the subassembly might have up to three possible suppliers with identical lead times but with different throughputs and costs. See Exhibit 8-3.

We defined *throughput* as the average output of a production process per unit time, while *capacity* was the upper limit on the throughput of a production process. As we already specified, supplier delivery uncertainty was a key issue that we wished to explore with the model. To explore this uncertainty, we introduce the concept of *"Quality Adjusted*

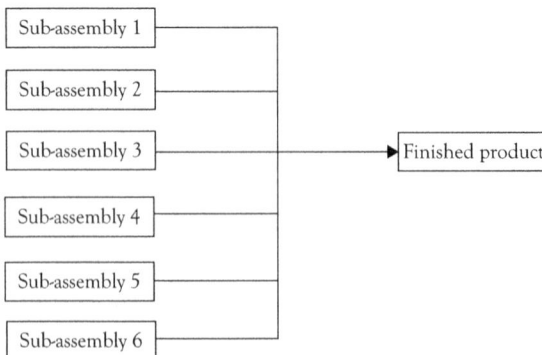

Exhibit 8-2. Bill of Materials of the Finished Product

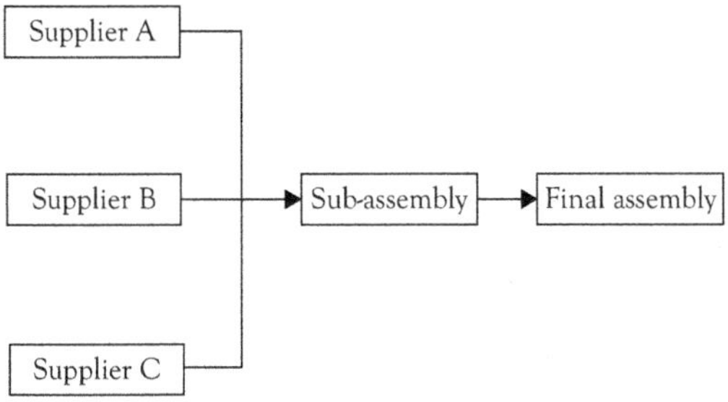

Exhibit 8-3. Three Suppliers per Sub-Assembly

Effective Capacity" (QAEC), which is the final, real, or observable monthly capacity after disruptions have occurred. To ease the analysis a bit we also assumed that suppliers for each component were independent and did not have knowledge of each other's capabilities and cost information. To make the model a bit more realistic, we added a non-delivery or shortage penalization cost at the final assembly stage and a second non-delivery or shortage penalization cost at the component stage. The idea here was to determine, in dollars, the cost of supply-chain delays and disruptions at both the subassembly and final assembly stages of the finished product.

Since the nominal capacity for each supplier would be affected by several, and different, random disruptions, plus the uncertainty associated with the final demand/consumption, suppliers were allowed to carry a safety stock of each component. Desiring to design a lean supply-chain operation, this safety stock would be used only when the supplier could not deliver the allocated order size. We also assumed that every component not delivered to the final assembly location would be lost (no backlogging allowed) and was penalized per occurrence. Every period, the supplier would produce the minimum of its capacity and its order size plus the difference between the on-hand inventory and the order-up-to level in case some material was consumed from the stock during the last period. Similarly, for each period, the inventory at the component stage would be the result of how much was produced plus the on-hand final inventory from the previous period, less the consumption at the final assembly area. This was the first stage of the two-stage stochastic process. Are you lost yet? All we are doing is looking at the suppliers of commodity materials to form the first five subassemblies and trying to identify the optimal number of components to be supplied by each and any associated buffer stocks. Referring back to the HLRM, if we were considering 500 units as the optimal number to have in final assembly, we wanted to know how the non-commodity parts and pieces of the 500 should be distributed across three different suppliers of these subassemblies for the lowest total cost. The QAEC was a measure of how well the supplier met our demands.

For the second stage, we assumed a similar structure for the final assembly operation, that is, each final assembly location was permitted to carry its own safety stock of its final product (obviously based on input from the previously discussed HLRM). However, the final production rate at each final assembly site would be a function of how many components were available, and its QAEC. In this case, the safety stock would buffer against the variability of its own final assembly operation (where its capacity was a random variable) and would also buffer against the variability at the supply stage and final demand. See Exhibit 8-4.

A simple example is now presented: Assume a supply chain with two components, three final assembly operations, three possible suppliers per component, and a monthly demand of 200 units. Exhibit 8-5 shows results for how each component units would be allocated to each supplier, and how total demand would be allocated to each final assembly operation. Therefore, supplier 1 for component 1 would produce 65 units every month of the total demand (or 32.6% of 200), while suppliers 2 and 3 would produce 87 and 47 units, respectively. The total sum for each

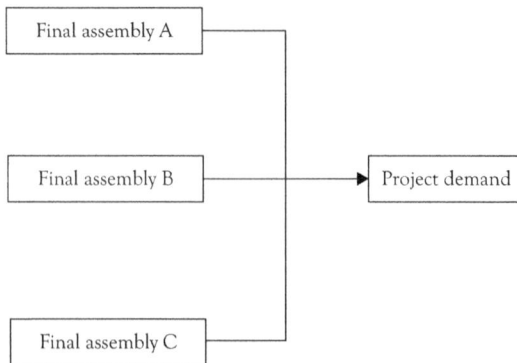

Exhibit 8-4. Three Final Assembly Sites to Satisfy Project Demand

Exhibit 8-5. Example with Three Final Assembly Sites, Two Components and Three Suppliers per Component

Component	Supplier	Diversification	Order size (units)
1	1	32.6%	65
	2	43.6%	87
	3	23.7%	47
2	1	50.3%	101
	2	49.7%	99
	3	0%	0
Final Assembly	1	70%	140
	2	15%	30
	3	15%	30

component is 100% (or 200 units). Similarly for final assembly sites 1, 2 and 3. This particular allocation represents the lowest total cost.

Two-Stage Decomposition

As we continued the development of the model, our decision to make the model a two-stage model was validated. By determining the QAEC of each of the targeted suppliers, we were able to determine when supplier stock-outs would drive shortages in the final assembly and thus were able to define appropriate buffer stocks for both suppliers and final assembly sites. Since the goal of the model was to minimize the total supply-chain system cost, which included production, inventory holding, and penalization costs at each supplier and the final assembly stage, we needed the ability to input "real-world" random variables, which were introduce capacity constraints into the model. In this model, the capacity parameters and final demand would random variables. To assist the decision maker, a user's interface was developed as shown in Exhibit 8-6.

The main model interface was divided into four sections as follows:

Section 1: Supplier's QAEC data–in this part, we determined the real average capacity and variability for each supplier. This capacity, as previously explained, was the result of the nominal capacity affected by possible disruptions. See Exhibit 8-7.

Exhibit 8-6. Business Allocation Model User's Interface

Project name			Target demand (units/month)			Delayed deployment cost ($ per unit)		
	Quality adjusted effective capacity (units/month)		Target allocation			Safety stock		
Suppliers	Mean (units)	Coefficient of variation	% Total	Monthly Q	Q units (mt)	SS Q	SS units (mt)	Service level
Sub Assembly 1				189.89	380,000	40.72	81,400	100%
Supplier 1	137.19	0.17	60.02%	113.96	228,000	34.19	68,400	100%
Supplier 2	88.8	0.11	39.98%	75.92	152,000	6.53	13,000	100%
Supplier 3	0.00	0.00	0%	0	0	0	0	100%
Sub Assembly 2			38.47%	194.93	390,000	12.87	25,700	100%
Supplier 1	70.57	0.51		75	150,000	0	0	100%
Supplier 2	98.49	0.10	48.27%	94.1	188,200	12.87	25,700	100%
Supplier 3	100	0.00	13.26%	25.85	51,700	0	0	100%
Sub Assembly 3				185.86	446,000	2.37	5,700	100%
Supplier 1	75.78	0.31	38.41%	71.38	171,000	1.51	3,600	100%
Supplier 2	58.95	0.30	19.65%	36.88	88,500	0.86	2,100	100%
Supplier.3	150.06	0.31	41.75%	77.59	186,000	0	0	100%

Sub Assembly 4				170	408,000	40.84	98,000	100%
Supplier 1	70.17	0.30	41.18%	70	168,000	0	0	100%
Supplier 2	50.17	0.40	29.41%	50	120,000	0	0	100%
Supplier 3	50.01	0.10	29.41%	50	120,000	40.84	98,000	100%
Sub Assembly 5				166.96	367,300	46.11	101,500	100%
Supplier 1	80.11	0.10	47.92%	80	176,000	0	0	100%
Supplier 2	30.00	0.00	17.97%	30	66,000	0	0	100%
Supplier 3	199.98	0.40	34.12%	56.96	125,300	46.11	101,500	100%
Final Assembly				150.5	150.5	0	0	100%
Site 1	1000.01	0.00	100%	150.5	150.5	0	0	100%
Site 2	0.00	0.00	0	0	0	0	0	0
Site 3	0.00	0.00	0	0	0	0	0	0
Actual demand	80	0.00						
Total monthly cost ($M)					Risk Analysis	Minimum cost	$400 M	100%
Production	$300	0.02				Maximum cost	$800 M	
Inventory holding	$200	0.01				Aspiration level	$700 M	
Delayed deployment	$100	0.03				Risk of exceeding aspiration level	43%	
Total	$600	0.02						

Exhibit 8-7. Quality-Adjusted Effective Capacity Section

	Quality-adjusted effective capacity	
Suppliers	**Mean (units)**	**Coefficient of variation**
Sub Assembly 1		
Supplier 1	137.19	0.17
Supplier 2	88.8	0.11
Supplier 3	0.00	0.00
Sub Assembly 2		
Supplier 1	70.57	0.51
Supplier 2	98.49	0.10
Supplier 3	100	0.00
Sub Assembly 3		
Supplier 1	75.78	0.31
Supplier 2	58.95	0.30
Supplier 3	150.06	0.01
Sub Assembly 4		
Supplier 1	70.17	0.30
Supplier 2	50.17	0.40
Supplier 3	50.01	0.10
Sub Assembly 5		
Supplier 1	80.11	0.10
Supplier 2	30.00	0.00
Supplier 3	199.98	0.40
Final Assembly		
Site 1	1000.01	0.00
Site 2	0.00	0.00
Site 3	0.00	0.00

Section 2: Diversification levels and safety stock–These columns showed the main output variables of the model (technically called first-stage variables): *diversification level and safety stock allocated to each supplier for each component.* For the diversification level, we had three values: % of total demand allocated to the supplier, lot size (in demand units and denoted by Q), and lot size in subassembly units (i.e., feet, pieces, etc.). In Exhibit 8-8, we observe that for a monthly demand of 150 fully assembled units, we had to order to order 191 units of subassembly 1 per month. That

Exhibit 8-8. Diversification Levels and Safety Stock Section

Suppliers	% Total	Monthly Q	Q Units (mt)	SS Q	SS Units (mt)	Service level
		Target allocation		Safety stock		
Sub Assembly 1 (total)		190.88	382,000	62.13	125,000	
Supplier 1	56.59%	108.02	216,000	43.82	88,000	100%
Supplier 2	43.41%	82.86	166,000	18.31	37,000	100%
Supplier 3	0%	0	0	0	0	100%
Sub Assembly 2 (total)		258.29	516,000	86.56	173,000	
Supplier 1	26.53%	68.53	137,000	67.4	135,000	100%
Supplier 2	38.72%	100	200,000	19.06	38,000	100%
Supplier 3	34.75%	89.76	179,000	0.1	192	100%
Sub Assembly 3 (total)		194.96	468,000	80.9	194,000	
Supplier 1	41.03%	80	192,000	44.65	107,000	99.63%
Supplier 2	29.16%	56.84	136,000	33.52	81,000	99.93%
Supplier 3	29.81%	58.11	140,000	2.72	6,500	100%
Sub Assembly 4 (total)		170	408,000	87.95	211,000	
Supplier 1	41.18%	70	168,000	40.02	96,000	96.93%
Supplier 2	29.41%	50	120,000	37.453	90,000	93.18%
Supplier 3	29.41%	50	120,000	10.5	25,000	99.98%
Sub Assembly 5 (total)		150.5	331,000	45.65	100,000	
Supplier 1	53.16%	80	176,000	20.4	45,000	83.7%
Supplier 2	19.93%	30	66,000	25.25	56,000	100%
Supplier 3	26.91%	40.5	89,000	0	0	99.88%
Final Assembly (total)		150.5	150.5	0	0	
Site 1	100%	150.5	150.5	0	0	0
Site 2	0	0	0	0	0	0
Site 3	0	0	0	0	0	0

monthly requirement was allocated in the following way: 108 demand units allocated to the first supplier, 83 demand units to the second, and nothing allocated to the third supplier. The next column shows the same allocation but in the subassembly 1 units. The fifth and sixth columns show the amount of safety stock required for each supplier. The service level that each supplier would provide as a function of its QAEC, lot size, and safety stock allocated is shown in the last column. The service level is the result of how many times the supplier was able to supply the allocated lot size (Q).

Both the order size (Q) and safety stock levels are the main variables to be optimized. However, the model also allowed the user to manually experiment with different levels of Q and safety stock. This kind of analysis provided an insight on how current or future non optimal strategies would impact total cost and service level.

Section 3: Service level and total cost–this section contained the two main performance components of the strategy: actual delivery and total monthly cost. Both of these metrics were the result of any specified diversification level and safety stock strategy (either optimal or manually set). *Actual delivery* included the expected monthly number of final product assemblies delivered, its associated variability, and expected service level. *Total monthly cost* was the total expected monthly system cost of the strategy and was the target variable to be minimized using Monte Carlo simulation. The total monthly cost was broken down in its three main elements: production, inventory holding, and delayed delivery. *Production cost* was the average cost incurred by the sourcing and assembly of all components. This amount was based on real quantities produced and not in production orders assigned. *Inventory holding cost* was the average cost incurred by keeping inventory during the planning horizon. This amount was based on how much inventory was kept at the end of the month for each supplier and its assembly operation. *Delayed delivery cost* was the average penalization incurred by any material stock-outs on components and/ or final assemblies. This penalization was based on the difference between the allocated production order and orders shipped. See Exhibit 8-9.

For the example given in Exhibit 8-9, the expected delivery of final assemblies per month is 199 units, with very little variability. This expected delivery resulted in a service level of 88.47%. The expected total cost per month of this strategy was $142 million.

Section 4: Risk analysis–the last component of the user's interface was a basic risk analysis feature. Because the model incorporated variability into

Exhibit 8-9. Service Level and Total Cost Section

Actual delivery	Mean	Coefficient of variation	Service level
Units per Month	198.82	0.02	88.47%
Total Monthly Cost ($M)			
Production Cost	140.52	0.02	
Inventory Holding Cost	0.2243	0.13	
Delayed Delivery Cost	1.3572	1.59	
Total	142.1	0.0207	

Exhibit 8-10. Risk Analysis Section

Risk Analysis (Total monthly cost in $M)	
Minimum Cost	128
Maximum Cost	170
Aspiration Level	143
Risk of Exceeding Aspiration Level	29.7%

the analysis and its objective was to minimize a random variable (total system cost), the result was not just the expected cost, but its complete probability distribution. Using the probability distribution for the total cost, a small amount of basic risk analysis was performed. The first two elements were the maximum and minimum cost of the allocation and inventory strategy (either optimal or set manually). These values provided an appropriate direction as to the best and worst case scenario for the total systems cost of a given supplier strategy. Using the results from Exhibit 8-9, we observe an expected cost of $142 million for a given allocation and inventory strategy; however, we could have the case of a "bad month" with a cost of $170 million as shown in Exhibit 8-10. The second component of this analysis was the probability assessment of exceeding a certain threshold or aspiration level. In Exhibit 8-10, we also observe that the probability or risk of exceeding a total monthly cost of $143 million is 29.7%.

The main user's interface allowed us to enter parameters for each assembly and the input variables for each supplier. Supplier input variables were selected via the supplier's capacity and cost parameters button on the user interface, and then selecting the supplier's information option.

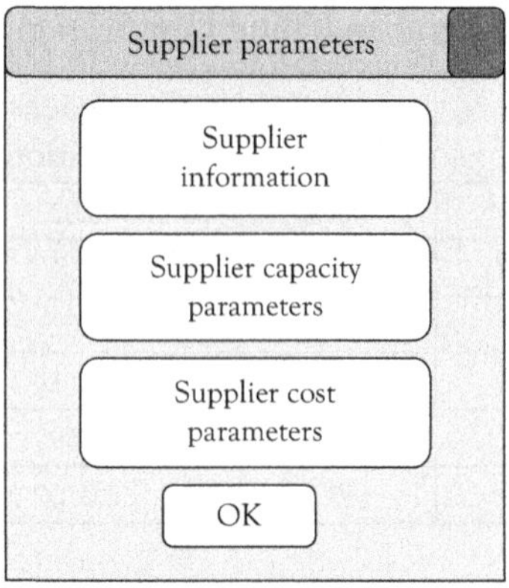

Exhibit 8-11A. Supplier Parameters Section

We then entered the name of potential suppliers for each component (including three options for the final assembly operation). See Exhibits 8-11A and 8-11B.

Data, Data, Data

Once each supplier was identified, the next step was to enter the cost structure for that supplier. For this set of parameters, we defined three main components. First, manufacturing cost: price quoted by each supplier, including material and labor. It is important to point out that all units had to have a common base unit, that is, $/foot, $/pound, $/gallon, and so on. Second, holding cost: the annual expense incurred by carrying inventory. This was usually expressed as a percentage of the average inventory investment. The typical range for this value was between 8% and 15% annually. Third, penalty cost: this was the cost incurred by all shortages, including final assemblies not delivered. Since each supplier was responsible to deliver a specified monthly quantity of components, they would be penalized for units not delivered. See Exhibit 8-12.

The next step was to identify supplier input variables. In this model, we assumed that the only two sources of variability were the supplier's monthly capacity and the final demand of the finished assembly. Although decision makers might have a good estimate of the average or expected final demand and nominal capacity for each supplier at component stage, these estimates could significantly change due to normal business variabil-

Exhibit 8-11B. Supplier Information Section

Supplier Information	
Component	**Manufacturer name**
Sub Assembly 1	
Manufacturer 1	ABC
Manufacturer 2	DEF
Manufacturer 3	GHI
Sub Assembly 2	
Manufacturer 1	ABC
Manufacturer 2	DEF
Manufacturer 3	GHI
Sub Assembly 3	
Manufacturer 1	ABC
Manufacturer 2	DEF
Manufacturer 3	GHI
Sub Assembly 4	
Manufacturer 1	ABC
Manufacturer 2	DEF
Manufacturer 3	GHI
Sub Assembly 5	
Manufacturer 1	ABC
Manufacturer 2	DEF
Manufacturer 3	GHI
Final Assembly	
Manufacturer 1	ABC
Manufacturer 2	DEF
Manufacturer 3	GHI
OK	

ity, equipment reliability, process yield, and external disruptions (usually called catastrophic events), such as strikes and natural disasters. Usually, practitioners are tempted to use simple averages on decision-making models ignoring any kind of uncertainty. However, as explained in the previous sections and largely mentioned in existing operations and supply chain literature, the risk of not considering variability in either supply or demand might drive to erroneous conclusions and poor system performance.

Exhibit 8-12. Supplier Cost Parameters Input Screen

Component	Manufacturer name	MFG cost ($/unit)	Unit (ea, ft, #)	Holding cost (%)	Penalty cost ($/unit)	Notes
Sub Assembly 1						
Manufacturer 1	ABC					
Manufacturer 2	DEF					
Manufacturer 3	GHI					
Sub Assembly 2						
Manufacturer 1	ABC					
Manufacturer 2	DEF					
Manufacturer 3	GHI					
Sub Assembly 3						
Manufacturer 1	ABC					
Manufacturer 2	DEF					
Manufacturer 3	GHI					
Sub Assembly 4						
Manufacturer 1	ABC					
Manufacturer 2	DEF					
Manufacturer 3	GHI					
Sub Assembly 5						
Manufacturer 1	ABC					
Manufacturer 2	DEF					
Manufacturer 3	GHI					
Final Assembly						
Manufacturer 1	ABC					
Manufacturer 2	DEF					
Manufacturer 3	GHI					
	OK					

We now introduce some detail in the procedure for the generation of scenarios. Starting from the main assumption that the monthly capacity for each supplier and the demand of final assemblies were random variables, we needed to generate data sets representing several months of capacity for each supplier at each component stage. We defined each scenario as a random combination of several uncertainty factors. In our case, each scenario was a sequence of 12 monthly possible capacity outcomes per supplier and 12 monthly demands. The sample size of $N = 500$ scenarios was defined to ensure that extreme events were captured. Four different kinds of variability were considered to define the expected effective capacity as follows:

1. **Normal variability**: the random fluctuations that the supplier's capacity would have under normal conditions. Gaussian (usually called "normal") and Gamma distributions with mean μ and coefficient of variation (CV) were used for modeling normal variability. In our case, we chose to define a random variable with low variability if its CV is less than 0.75, moderate variability if its CV is between 0.75 and 1.33, and high variability if the CV is greater than 1.33.

2. **Supplier reliability**: any kind of disruption that the supplier would have because of any factor under its control, such as machine failure, maintenance, labor strikes, and raw material supply (internal factors). In this case, any kind of shutdown at the supplier would have a certain number of effective production days lost. This would impact the nominal capacity already affected by normal fluctuations. For this kind of disruption, we used the concept of *mean time between failures* (MTBF), which is the average time elapsed between two consecutive failures. A reasonable assumption was to use an exponential distribution to model the time between failures. A second parameter to represent the duration of the failure, or how long it would take to repair, was the *mean time to repair* (MTTR), which is defined as the average time that a device will take to recover from a non-terminal failure. Similar to MTBF, an exponential distribution was used to model the time to repair failures.

3. **Process yield**: defined as the average percentage of good parts produced each month. A binomial distribution was used to model the behavior of the process yield. A sequence of independent Bernoulli trials was used to generate the number of good parts per month.

4. **Catastrophic events or acts of God**: these were the kind of disruptions out of the control of the supplier (also known as external

factors): snow storms, flooding, earthquakes, and so on. Like the supplier reliability, any shutdowns because of a catastrophic event would affect the nominal capacity. The procedure to model this kind of disruption is similar to the one used for supplier reliability; therefore, an exponential distribution was used for both the inter-arrival time of disruptions and their duration.

The final or effective capacity that the supplier would have every period (month) would be the result of the normal variability, supplier reliability, process yield, and catastrophic events. Because the service level at the final assembly plants was subject to the supplier's performance, the main challenge was how to allocate the order size given that every supplier was subject to all these forms of disruptions. The combination of the above four kinds of variability is what we called Quality Adjusted Effective Capacity (QAEC). See Exhibit 8-13.

Regarding nominal capacity, we defined it as the theoretical monthly capacity only subject to normal variability, without any kind of internal or external disruptions. For nominal capacity, we assumed a Gaussian probability distribution when the CV is below 0.2 and a Gamma distribution when the CV is above 0.2. The reason for doing this was that in the case of Gaussian distributions, "negative capacities" can be generated when the CV exceeds 0.2.

For supplier reliability, once the nominal capacity for a given month had been sampled from the Gaussian or Gamma distributions, the next step was sampling for the number of days the supplier would lose from

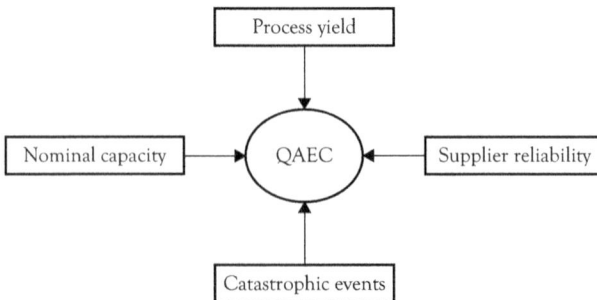

Exhibit 8-13. *Quality Adjusted Effective Capacity (QAEC)*

its nominal capacity each month. The two parameters required here were previously mentioned: MTBF and MTTR. Assuming exponential inter-arrival times of failures with mean MTBF, we also computed the probability of not having a failure from the first to the last month of the year (scenario) using the Poisson distribution.

Accounting for catastrophic events was quite challenging. Since machine and equipment breakdowns are not the only source of capacity disruptions, as previously described, external factors such as strikes, natural disasters, sabotages, and extreme situations like terrorist attacks are other sources of disruption that must be considered. Based on managerial input, we identified ten different categories of catastrophic events as follows:

- Tornado
- Earthquake
- Flood
- Snow Storm
- Hurricane
- Labor Strike
- Terrorist Attack
- Sabotage
- Health, safety, security and environmental (HSSE)
- Other

For sampling purposes, we followed an approach similar to the one we used for supplier reliability. However, in the case of catastrophic events, we had ten possible sources of interruption, each with a different duration. We assigned a probability of occurrence to each event based on its frequency and an associated duration. See Exhibit 8-14.

For process yield, our assumption was that no manufacturing process is 100% reliable in terms of good parts; therefore, it was necessary to include this source of uncertainty into scenario generation. Using the average value of good parts for each supplier, we followed the procedure of inverting the binomial distribution based on a sequence of independent Bernoulli trials. Once all supplier information had been entered, a macro was then run to execute the sampling algorithms.

Exhibit 8-14. *Catastrophic Events Input Screen*

Catastrophic events for final assembly 2		
Enter how often this type of catastrophic event occurs in which the manufacturing facility would face a shutdown or closure. For example, the facility may be located where there are many winter snowstorms, however, a plant shutdown due to snowstorms may occur only once every 2 years; therefore enter a "2" in the dialog box.		
Catastrophic events	**Frequency** (on average, this event occurs once every "X" years)	**Mean duration** (on average, this event lasts "X" days)
Tornado ☐		
Earthquake ☐		
Flood ☐		
Snow Storm ☐		
Hurricane ☐		
Labor Strike ☐		
Terrorist Attack ☐		
Sabotage ☐		
Health, Safety, Security, Environmental ☐		
Other ☐		
OK		

After having entered all suppliers' capacity parameters, the next step was to define the parameters for the consumption of final assemblies. Although we expected low variation on the quantity of final assemblies required every month, any little change on the mean target might have a significant impact on the total performance of the system. For modeling purposes, we assumed a Gamma distribution to generate consumption for final assemblies. As noted previously, we identified two main parameters: mean monthly demand and coefficient of variation (CV). If we did not expect any kind of variability, we would set the $CV = 0$. In actuality, we did not expect more than 20% variability. Exhibit 8-16 shows a simple table with equivalent CV for different levels of variability.

Once the user had entered all the consumption information, the *sampling for demand* button called another macro that contained the sampling algorithm that would generate a sample of 500 years of monthly demand.

Parameters for Final Assembly			
Mean Capacity (final assemblies/month)	150	C.V.	0.01
Mean Time Between Failures (months)	10000	Mean Time To Repair (days)	0.05
Quality Yield (decimal)	0.95		
Change Catastrophic Event Parameters		Sample for Quality Adjusted Effective Capacity	
	OK		

Exhibit 8-15. Process Yield Input Screen

Demand Parameters			
Mean Target Demand (final assemblies/month)	150	Note for C.V.: use 0.0166 for ± 5%, 0.0333 for ± 10%, 0.05 for ± 15%, or 0.0667 for ± 20%	
C.V.	0.05		
	Sample for Demand		
	OK		

Exhibit 8-16. Project Demand Input Screen

Getting Something to Work and Understanding Results

Once all the input parameters had been entered and all scenarios had been generated, the next step was optimization of the order size and safety stock allocation for each component supplier. This step could be done in two different ways: manually or by using the optimization algorithm. Using the manual approach, the user could modify the individual values for the levels of production and safety stock. Each time any of the decision variables was changed, the monthly expected delivery and total cost was updated. This approach was helpful if the user wanted to explore the impact of future strategies on the monthly expected delivery and total cost.

Since the trial and error approach of manually entering various input data would be time consuming because of the number of variables and combinations possible, the model incorporated an optimization algorithm. By clicking the optimization button, a macro with the optimization algorithm was executed. This algorithm first generated a set of feasible starting points for the order size, and using this starting solution, a spreadsheet "solver" function was called to find the optimal solution. This methodology also generated a starting solution for the safety stock using a heuristic approach. Again, after setting an initial solution, the solver was called to find the optimal safety stocks. If the user changed some parameters after the optimization was complete, the optimization procedure was then repeated. It is also important to point out that due to the nature of the model being nonlinear and because of the heuristic approach to generate starting solutions, optimality of the solution could not be guaranteed. What the model provided was an overall direction to proceed in pursuing a particular strategy with a supplier.

To test this model, and to gain some additional understanding as to the impact of supplier diversification, we developed two numerical problem instances to help illustrate the impact of supplier diversification in complex supply-chain structures. For each problem instance, we first applied what we call "common sense" when selecting suppliers. Then, we used the optimization procedure to find the best supplier selection and order allocation. By doing this comparison, we showed the risk of supplier selection by just considering nominal capacity and cost structure. To simplify our analysis in this numerical example, we did not consider catastrophic events for any supplier and we assumed deterministic consumption with a coefficient of variation of zero.

For the first example, we used a target demand of 100 units/month (no variability) with a penalization of $500,000 for every unit not delivered to the deployment site and a penalization of $50,000 for every component stock-out. The parameters for each supplier are shown in Exhibit 8-17.

By only considering nominal mean capacity and production cost, "common sense" would indicate that 100% of the demand (or an order of 100 units per month) would be allocated to the cheapest supplier for each component, since all the suppliers had a capacity greater than the order size of 100 units. By using the sampling procedure with the rest of the supplier's information, we generated scenarios of possible QAEC outcomes to analyze the impact of the previous allocation decision. See Exhibit 8-18.

Exhibit 8-17. First Example of the Business Allocation Model

Assembly	Suppliers	Nominal		Reliability		Quality	Cost		
		Mean	C.V.	MTBF	MTTR	Quality (%)	Prod ($K)	Holding (%)	Penalty ($K)
Sub-assembly 1	Supplier 1	100	0.2	4	2	98	18.4	25	50
	Supplier 2	120	0.3	2	2	96	16.6	25	50
	Supplier 3	120	0.0	100,000	0	100	20.2	25	50
Sub-assembly 2	Supplier 1	250	0.3	6	10	98	120	25	50
	Supplier 2	100	0.2	9	12	99	108	25	50
	Supplier 3	50	0.01	12	2	100	132	25	50
Sub-assembly 3	Supplier 1	150	0.01	100,000	0	100	59	25	50
	Supplier 2	150	0.01	100,000	0	100	53.1	25	50
	Supplier 3	150	0.01	100,000	0	100	64.9	25	50
Sub-assembly 4	Supplier 1	50	0.2	10	4	99	92.4	25	50
	Supplier 2	100	0.25	5	2	98	83.1	25	50
	Supplier 3	110	0.02	100,000	0	100	101.6	25	50
Sub-assembly 5	Supplier 1	150	0.01	100,000	0	100	53.8	25	50
	Supplier 2	150	0.01	100,000	0	100	58.4	25	50
	Supplier 3	150	0.01	100,000	0	100	59.1	25	50
Final assembly	Site 1	150	0.01	100,000	0	100	46	25	50
	Site 2	150	0.01	100,000	0	100	41.4	25	50
	Site 3	150	0.01	100,000	0	100	50.6	25	50

Exhibit 8-18. "Common Sense" Allocation

Actual delivery	Mean	Coefficient of variation	Service level
Units per Month	78.64	0.18	10.23%
Total Monthly Cost ($M)			
Production Cost	81.7	0.05	
Inventory Holding Cost	–	–	
Delayed Delivery Cost	12.1635	0.60	
Total	93.87	0.0592	
Risk analysis (Total monthly cost in $M)			
Minimum Cost	86.45		
Maximum Cost	125.79		
Aspiration Level	90		
Risk of Exceeding Aspiration Level	73.3%		

Exhibit 8-18 demonstrates the result of applying the "common sense" allocation. In this case, the expected monthly delivery is 78.64 units, with a service level of 10.23% (in only 10.23% of the 500 scenarios was the system able to deliver a complete order of 100 units). The expected monthly cost of this allocation was $93.87 million. The risk analysis table shows the maximum and minimum monthly cost obtained. Since the cost of the allocation was a random variable, we could easily compute the probability (or risk) of exceeding a certain threshold or aspiration cost. In this example, we set the aspiration level to $90 million, with an associated risk of exceeding it calculating out at 73.3%.

Since the expected delivery rate, total monthly cost, and risk involved for this allocation were not acceptable, we proceeded to use the optimization procedure to find the best order size and safety stock allocation at the minimum cost. The result of the optimization procedure is shown in Exhibit 8-19.

In this case, by changing the allocation and safety stock strategy, we improved the expected delivery rate from 78.64 final assemblies per month to 99.85 final assemblies per month with a service level of 97.73% versus 10.23% from the previous, "common sense" solution. The expected total monthly cost was reduced from $93.87 million to $87.83 million, and the risk of exceeding the aspiration level of $90 million was reduced from

Exhibit 8-19. Optimal Allocation

Actual delivery	Mean	Coefficient of variation	Service level
Units per Month	99.85	0.01	97.73%
Total Monthly Cost ($M)			
Production Cost	87.33	0.03	
Inventory Holding Cost	0.3622	0.11	
Delayed Delivery Cost	0.1305	5.44	
Total	87.83	0.0279	
Risk analysis (Total monthly cost in $M)			
Minimum Cost	76.91		
Minimum Cost	99.02		
Aspiration Level	90		
Risk of Exceeding Aspiration Level	16.3%		

73.3% to 16.3%. The optimization procedure also revealed that the order size should be allocated to two suppliers, with the first supplier being allocated at 51% and the second at 49%. In addition, the second supplier was expected to carry a safety stock of 60 units, equivalent to 1 month of production while supplier 1 was responsible for 27 units in inventory every month. Additionally, allocation of other components were identified, and, as expected, for those suppliers having little or no-variability, the least expensive supplier was allocated 100% of the allocation of the order. From the optimization perspective, this is the best strategy.

We also point out some important aspects of this numerical example. First, the risk incurred by using "common sense" or simple approaches to define the best allocation and inventory strategy is just that, a simple approach. Even if all suppliers had capacity above the target demand, the impact of different sources of variability affects the real performance of each supplier. Second, with the optimal strategy, we were able to improve the expected delivery and service level with a lower expected cost compared with the simple allocation. Third, the numbers in and of themselves are not that important. What is important here is that insight was given to each of the each supplier's capabilities and capacities, and the impact of random business interruptions are not insignificant. Directionally, this information would be used to negotiate with a supplier, not just on price, but on reducing variation from many sources, improving service levels, and perhaps even enabling some learning curve capture as variations are reduced.

As with all models, one must be prepared to perform some extensive troubleshooting. Exhibit 8-20 demonstrates the results of one particular scenario that 100% guaranteed that the aspirational levels would be exceeded and that the maximum cost could be up to $25 billion per month. Obviously there was a mistake somewhere and we include the example here just as a reminder that it takes significant effort, rigor, and discipline to develop excellent models. They will generate a few headaches along the way!

Final Thoughts

As we have mentioned before, the main objective of the Business Allocation Model was not to propose efficient sampling and optimization algorithms, but rather to offer a general framework for the strategic design of supply chains in the presence of stochastic supply disruptions within the framework of moving new products out of R&D and into commercialization.

To conclude this chapter, we want to reiterate a few points. The HLRM was developed to provide insight as to the number of final assemblies held in inventory to account for variations in deployment. If you remember, this was important as the final assembly was not going to be marketed by the company but would be consumed by another business unit within the company. Our concern was to be directionally correct given the relative immaturity of the supply-chain development program. Precision would come as further details were developed and passed out of R&D to the commercial team. With respect to the BAM, we needed to gain understanding and insight into how supplier disruptions would impact the amount of business allocated to each supplier. Given the supplier relationships developed by R&D, it was extremely important that the R&D folks understand a supplier's capability and capacity to meet requirements from not only a technical point of view, but also a commercial point of view. The results of this modeling exercise clearly demonstrated the magnitude of the risk incurred by the company should exclusive supplier

Exhibit 8-20. Second Example of the Business Allocation Model

Project name		Target demand (units/month)				Delayed deployment cost ($ per unit)			
	Quality adjusted effective capacity (units/month)		Target allocation				Safety stock		
Suppliers	Mean (units)	Coefficient of variation	% Total	Monthly Q	Q units (mt)		SS Q	SS Units (mt)	Service level (%)
Sub-assembly 1				118.21	236,000		86	172,000	
Supplier 1	95.56	0.21	49.58	58.61	117,000		27	52,000	100
Supplier 2	111.13	0.30	50.42	59.6	119,000		59	120,000	100
Supplier 3	120	0.00	0.00	0.00	0		0	0	100
Sub-assembly 2				122.49	245,000		7	14,000	
Supplier 1	222.31	0.38	18.36	22.49	45,000		7	14,000	98.4
Supplier 2	97.03	0.21	81.64	100	200,000		0	0	94.4
Supplier 3	49.65	0.02	0.00	0.00	0		0	0	100
Sub-assembly 3				100.5	240,000		0	0	
Supplier 1	149.98	0.01	0.00	0	0		0	0	100
Supplier 2	149.99	0.01	100	100.5	240,000		0	0	100
Supplier 3	149.99	0.01	0.00	0.00	0		0	0	100

(Continued)

Suppliers	Mean (units)	Coefficient of variation	% Total	Monthly Q	Q units (mt)	SS Q	SS Units (mt)	Service level (%)
Sub-assembly 4				127.74	300,000	11	25,000	
Supplier 1	47.75	0.22	21.72	27.74	65,000	11	25,000	99.9
Supplier 2	95.91	0.26	78.28	100	235,000	0	0	93.6
Supplier 3	109.98	0.02	0.00	0.00	0	0	0	100
Sub-assembly 5				100.5	220,000	0	10	
Supplier 1	149.97	0.01	0.00	0.00	0	0	0	100
Supplier 2	149.96	0.01	100	100.5	220,000	0	10	100
Supplier 3	149.98	0.01	0.00	0.00	0	0	0	100
Final Assembly				100.5	100.5	0	0	
Site 1	149.98	0.01	0.00	0.00	0	0	0	100
Site 2	149.99	0.01	100	100.5	100.5	0	0	97.7
Site 3	150	0.01	0.00	0.00	0	0	0	100
Actual Demand	70	0.00						100 %
Total monthly cost ($M)				Risk analysis				
Production	$591.6	0.58				Minimum cost	$786 M	
Inventory holding	$200.6	0.01				Maximum cost	$25,000 M	
Delayed deployment	$0.00013	77.46				Aspiration level	$500 M	
Total	$792.25	0.433				Risk of exceeding aspiration level	100%	

relationships be permitted and how diversification of the supplier base mitigated this risk. By providing this sort of information as feedback to R&D, they in turn would be able to tailor their engagement with alternative suppliers and establish appropriate expectations with suppliers as the relationship developed. The last point we would make regarding this modeling exercise is that it could, and was, used within the context of a "supplier war game" that we developed to test the supply-chain strategy for a critical component. Chapter 11 describes the "supplier war game."

CHAPTER 9

Supplier Networking

Many books have been written on the subject of supplier networking, and our intention is to boil the subject down to some bare essentials. Supplier networking is an easy concept to discuss, but an extremely difficult topic to navigate. In our case, we knew that our project had some quite unique characteristics, and it was up to us to determine how we could best leverage those project characteristics in the supply chain. We also had some fairly grandiose ideas, like we should be able to START with a supply-chain network that resembled Boeing's or Toyota's. Well, as you can imagine, that was truly a dumb idea.

Considering the unique qualities of our overall project and specific technology, the characteristics we were primarily interested in leveraging with suppliers were:

- long-life of the project (30+ years)
- constant and stable demand
- single customer (us)
- really only one stock keeping unit (SKU)
- learning curve capture

We wished to extract value out of our supply chain to maintain competitive advantage and considered the best approach to doing that was:

- concentrating our supplier base
- issuing contracts that rewarded value creation and sharing
- open-book collaboration with suppliers
- joint performance tracking and planning
- dedicated teams to manage the networks

Why?

So why did we even start down this path? Well, if you really boil it all down, given all of the unique characteristics of this effort, we believed the long life of the project would enable us to develop a close-knit network of key, long-term suppliers and buyers that would work closely together to deliver an optimized value chain. Having joint incentives, opening books, and sharing knowledge, coupled with having few SKUs, a sole customer, and stable demand should have been quite compelling toward attracting suppliers into the network. Collaboration between the entities would increase the cost savings across everyone's value chains. Buyers for the firm would capture greater value through value sharing provisions in contracts while suppliers would earn superior margins as they met network goals and integrated best practices of the total network, so we thought.

We recognized that supplier networks differed by the amount of collaboration between suppliers and clients. While our firm was well-disciplined and experienced with respect to traditional, transactional-based relationships, it had no experience achieving deep, long-term supplier relationships where there was significant knowledge sharing and interaction among the suppliers. In addition, sharing of intellectual property, open-book collaboration, and so on, was quite another matter. To approach this issue, we again performed some qualitative assessments to determine where in our supply chain we were most suited toward arms-length, market-based competition to reduce costs and where it was necessary for long-term collaboration for cost reduction, innovation, and quality improvements. Exhibit 9-1 demonstrates this evaluation.

Traveling down this path of collaborative supplier networks therefore required us to have great understanding of the breadth and depth of the network we were trying to establish. It was imperative that there be a joint focus on value that a clear definition would exist for the degree and amount of collaboration and information sharing, and most importantly, a strong dedicated leadership committed to the success of the overall supplier network was required. To that end, we set out to study the supply networks established by Wal-Mart, Boeing, and Toyota to understand the implications on our supply chain should we choose to adopt their network model or a hybrid thereof.

Exhibit 9-1. Supplier Networking Qualitative Assessment

Criteria	Traditional arms-length relationship	Collaborative supplier network relationship
Importance of "End-to-End" Value Chain Optimization	Value chain optimization occurs through competition	Inventories and leadtimes can be significantly reduced through collaboration
Technical/ Manufacturing Process Maturity	Little need for R & D and learning	Continual need for learning, product development, process improvements, etc.
Intellectual Property Considerations	Limited IP risks, mature products	Proprietary processes and know-how are crucial
Number, Capability, and Capacity of Qualified Suppliers	Short contracts and frequent rebids foster competition and reduce costs	Long-term contracts focused on value creation and sharing to jointly create value
Product Complexity	Little product differentiation, competing primarily on price	Product complexity offers large innovation opportunities
Proportion of Learning Value Through the Network	Competition forces suppliers to pass value to customer	Manage supplier power by "locking-in" relationships
Risk of Supply Shortage	Many suppliers with low switching costs between suppliers	Limited number of suppliers creates heavily dependent relationships

Balance

Considerations

The results of our study indicated that there was significant opportunity to establishing some sort of collaborative supplier network. While there was a high base cost for the product, there was also ample opportunity for cost savings through innovation and collaboration. There were no suppliers that had the capability and capacity to meet commercial project requirements and the firm's manufacturing capacities were also insufficient to support a large-scale project. There was opportunity to accelerate the learning curve while protecting intellectual property if we engaged in a collaborative relationship early and "locked-in" our key suppliers. In turn, our suppliers would experience fairly low-risk growth while being allowed to apply practices developed with us to reduce their production costs and increase margins on products manufactured for other customers. We saw

Exhibit 9-2. A "Gives" and "Gets" Analysis Between the Firm and Network Suppliers

	"Gives"	"Gets"
Firm	Steady and stable demand, concentrated supplier base, best practice sharing, superior margins, network costs.	Portion of network savings. Responsive supply chain. Greater IP protection.
Network Suppliers	Exclusive relationship, open—book financials, best practice sharing with network partners.	Best-in-class margins, low risk growth, learning and application of processes to non-competitive customers.

tremendous opportunity in being able to outsource production using supplier networks, but the next question we needed to answer centered around making an appropriate business case for our targeted suppliers.

Referring back to Exhibit 9-1, almost every criterion was balanced heavily toward adopting the supplier network concept. However, to build the business case around the supplier network concept, we really needed to determine, from a high-level, "who" was "giving" and "getting" "what." Exhibit 9-2 demonstrates our approach.

To that end, we recognized that our network contracts would be a blend of traditional, arms-length contracts, and something more. In specific terms, contracts with our network suppliers would be required to address the following:

- Basic financial agreement
  - Pricing method
  - Starting price
  - Duration (including any renewal options)
  - Payment methods and timing
  - Renegotiation rights
  - Non-performance clauses
  - Other pricing factors (commodity cost fluctuations, regulatory requirements, vendor-managed inventory, etc.)
- Basic performance agreement
  - Product description
  - Specifications and technical data
  - Quality Assurance/Quality Control requirements

- ○ Volume
- ○ Delivery schedules and methods
- ○ Termination rights
- ○ Other standard contract provisions
- Network supplier financial incentives
  - ○ Firm retains all "unique" characteristics savings
  - ○ Time-based price reductions
  - ○ Supplier bonus structures
  - ○ Payment of network and data management costs
- Network supplier performance requirements
  - ○ Exclusivity
  - ○ Confidentiality
  - ○ Employee non-compete agreements
  - ○ Intellectual property ownership
  - ○ Sharing of performance metrics
  - ○ Network collaboration requirements
  - ○ Network management
  - ○ Volume adjustments

As previously stated, we also knew that a clear definition would be required for the degree and amount of collaboration and information sharing, and that, most importantly, a strong dedicated leadership committed to the success of the overall supplier network was required. Regarding collaboration and information sharing, there were three principal areas that needed to be well-managed.

1. **Network-wide interactions**

   Information shared would be general in nature and would focus on industry best practices, coordinating network issues, production scheduling, and monitoring overall network performance.

2. **Dedicated firm–supplier interactions**

   These interactions focused on collaboration between the firm and supplier R&D personnel in development of technology, practices, procedures, requirements, specifications, and other technical information. Appropriate processes would be in place for proper attribution of intellectual property as the teams worked together.

3. **Supplier–supplier interactions**

These interactions focused primarily on industry best practice sharing between suppliers, leveraging common areas as much as possible, and maintaining data and information integrity flowing between the suppliers.

Open Books? Really?

The idea of supplier "open books" started out as a noble idea but became completely untenable for implementation. It is easy to understand why. The firm was asking suppliers to open their financial books and documentation and had no intention of opening its own. No supplier wished to place themselves in a position where their customer was going to render a judgment regarding the margins they were obtaining. They viewed themselves as always being required to explain, "Why are you making so much money?"

So why did we believe in the network concept? Simply put, we believed that the unique characteristics of the project would speak for themselves and that suppliers would be flocking to participate. We believed that there was more than enough to go around for everyone. We believed, within our own organization, that the innovation and creativity of the technology, coupled with the necessity to drive down costs and capture learning curve benefits, was sufficient to cause a change in the methodology of our standardized contracting and procurement practices. Well, as we continued to develop the project and our supply-chain approach, our research results of all our suppliers certainly challenged our belief system.

KISS (we all know what this means right?)

At this point in the book, we think it is really important to make a strong recommendation. While it is appropriate to "begin with the end in mind," it is much more important to keep things simple when getting started. The reality of our situation did not warrant this level of supplier networking analysis. Was the research interesting? Yes. Practical? No. Why? Because of execution. Toyota, Boeing, Wal-Mart, and so on, did not arrive at their present day supply chains overnight. It was presumptuous of us to believe that we could set up a hybrid strategy based on the supply chains of these companies at the very start of the project, when we could not even obtain the full co-operation and buy-in of a single supplier to get the first commercial product out the door on time. Yes, it was a target to shoot for, but we were making it far too difficult. Don't do that. Go slow, establish one relationship at a time. KEEP IT SIMPLE…END OF STORY.

CHAPTER 10

Decision Framing

Decision framing is a very interesting topic and is a subject worthy of significant attention in its own right. The reason we bring it up is that sooner or later, some difficult decisions may need to be taken with respect to the supply-chain development program, which will result in significant dollars being expended. Decision framing is simply another tool that will assist decision makers in gaining additional levels of assurance and greater understanding of the primary focus issues of the project.

We have no intention of going into the nuts and bolts of decision framing and analysis. There are many consultants who can and will help with this sort of thing. The trick is to find someone who will train your folks on how to do it themselves to get an even bigger bang for the buck. What we will do is really just have a high-level review of a decision framing exercise that we went through and show the primary result.

As you may recall, we decided to take a "make" decision regarding the final manufacturing and assembly of the R&D product. The supplier base was constrained, and the firm was unwilling to put forth a business case to the few suppliers willing to be involved with us at a risk level they could tolerate. So the decision was made to "make" the final product and with that decision came an entire host of new questions. Build a plant? Yes. Wow!

What would be the scope of the plant? Where would it be located? Who would own the plant? Who would operate? When would the plant be ready? You kind of get the idea. The immediate issue that we had to deal with was that the plant needed to be built and go into production about a year or so before the rest of the multi-billion dollar project was going to be ready. The R&D folks were still busy perfecting the technology to be commercialized and, at the same time, were making significant strides on the next-generation technology. The primary questions of management were cost, scope, and ownership/operatorship. We chose to use the decision framing tool to help us answer these questions.

Getting Started with Decision Framing

The first order of business in developing a decision frame is to ensure that the correct question is being asked. This question needs to be sufficiently broad, yet concise. In our case, the decision question was, "Given that no infrastructure for building the product exists today to meet target costs and land is being purchased to build a manufacturing facility, what type of manufacturing plant is the best to deliver low-cost, reliable products, which meet initial project financial targets?"

Once the decision question is identified, and most importantly, agreed to by the group, it is then necessary to specifically identify key focus questions the decision frame needs to address. For example, "What is the best way to mass produce the product?," "What is the best way to capture the learning curve?," "What is the best way to gain industry assistance?" and so on. It is important to note that these key focus questions need to be kept to a minimum, 5 to 6 at the most, as digging deeper with increasingly smaller amounts of definitive information has a tendency to derail the decision framing process. The idea here is to establish a hierarchy of issues that can be used to advance the discussion further.

As the decision framing process is started, it is important to segregate issues. We differentiated issues with respect to "here and now" type decisions, strategic versus tactical decisions, facts, givens, assumptions, business goals, and so on. Given all of the issues that are offered up in the decision framing process, the most important aspect of getting started is to ensure that everyone working with the decision frame is operating off the same set of givens and assumptions. Without this initial alignment, the frame can quickly get out of control. As issues are categorized, it becomes clear that a decision pyramid could be constructed, which had business goal type issues at the top of the pyramid and facts at the base of the pyramid. A sanity check of the pyramid can then be performed to ensure that the key focus questions are contained within the decision pyramid.

Once issues have been well identified, the next step is to approach the frame from a high-level perspective and formulate some different strategies for answering the primary decision question. To formulate strategies, the focus decisions are used to assist in sorting the strategies from each other. In our case, plant capacity and product architectures were two of the focus decisions that were used to assist in sorting strategies. The strategies were then laid out in a spreadsheet in a matrix format with strategies in a column and focus decisions running in a row. Differentiating elements for each strategy were then identified, and a qualitative analysis was performed to identify a strategy to perform quantitative analysis. It is not as hard as it sounds (just hard to describe).

Identifying a Winning Strategy

One strategy we chose was called the "CEO Plan." The objective of this strategy was to improve the overall economics of the project using the next-generation technology, which had a lower overall cost (it was just taking a lot of time to get it proven out and we were still 3 to 4 years away from prime time). The rationale behind the strategy was that it was the next best alternative to the current technology. The problem with this strategy was that it did nothing for us now in terms of delivering products to the commercial project.

Another strategy we developed was called the "Flexible Plant" strategy. Its objective was to start with the technology we had, but to build the plant in such a way as to accommodate future product development. The primary rationale behind this strategy was capturing learning and having production flexibility. We had analyzed this strategy before in terms of lowest possible risk, so it made sense to evaluate the strategy quantitatively as well. In all, nine different strategies were developed, including one that we called "Outsource Everything" (which was really nothing more than the virtual plant strategy we have previously discussed). The idea here was to identify appropriate strategies that we could expeditiously execute in a straightforward fashion to deliver products to the field at lowest possible cost.

Once strategies were identified, we then engaged in a mapping exercise to determine, which strategies best met with the focus decisions. Here is how this worked. Imagine you have a decision question of having sufficient energy for the day. You have a strategy of "eat three meals" and you have focus decisions consisting only of breakfast, lunch, and dinner. Under each of these focus decisions, you had a series of options, for example, breakfast had the options of cereal, fruit, pancakes, and other off the grill. The idea is that for each strategy, you would pick the "menu" options, which best fit the strategy you were working on. In our case, for the focus area of product architecture, we had menu options of "current technology only," "current technology plus all others presently on drawing board," "all other technologies except for current technology," "start with current technology and then do change-outs to follow-ons," and "start with next generation technology and then move to other follow-ons afterward." As each strategy was qualitatively assessed against the focus areas, we would mark each of the menu items as to where the strategy would work. At the end of the day, and it was truly at least one solid day of work to do the strategy matrix (and everyone's head will hurt at the end of it—we guarantee it), the matrix of strategies would have then been completed. Compiling the results of what strategies worked where, we observed that some strategies simply fell off table as not being feasible. Among them was the "outsource everything–virtual plant" strategy. Others very quickly rose to the top as being serious contenders for quantitative analysis. The rigor and discipline of the decision framing process simply identified the top strategies with the highest probability of success for implementation. More importantly, those strategies that had little to no probability of success were eliminated, and *everyone involved* knew *why*. This is huge since the multi-disciplinary team constructing the strategy matrix will flow the results of the analysis back through their individual departments, thereby helping keep all departments on the same page.

Once strategies have been defined, it then becomes a relatively straightforward activity to start developing economic models around each of the top strategies. It is extremely important to keep these economic models simple and at a high level. Remember, our product would only be used within our firm and that our costs would really be a transfer cost between our Division and the Operations Division. We were not selling the product on the open market and thus what we were really interested in was the cost to this particular division of the firm. So our economic model needed to reflect product cost in this manner. We selected a metric of "net present cost" to the overall project as the variable that we would develop our economic models around.

Our Results

We will not go into any further detail with respect to any of the particular strategies that we considered or the associated cost models developed for the selected strategies, but we will simply show the output of the analysis in Exhibit 10-1. The take-away here is that there was clearly a winning strategy which presented the lowest total cost to the project as a whole. There was also a clearly "losing" strategy. There were other strategies that were extremely similar in their cost profiles. In our case, the clear loser was the "outsource everything–virtual plant" strategy, whereas the clear winner was the strategy that was based on the next-generation technology that would not be available for about 4 years.

So now that we had some numbers to work with (and also knowing that humans are notorious for our inability to accurately estimate), we revisited the decision question: "Given that no infrastructure for building products exists today to meet target costs and land is being purchased to build a manufacturing facility, what type of manufacturing plant is the best to deliver low-cost, reliable products to meet initial project cost targets?" The "answer" to the question was to proceed with the "Flexible Plant" strategy (this strategy was represented by one of the curves in the middle of Exhibit 10-1). This strategy met our project timing requirements

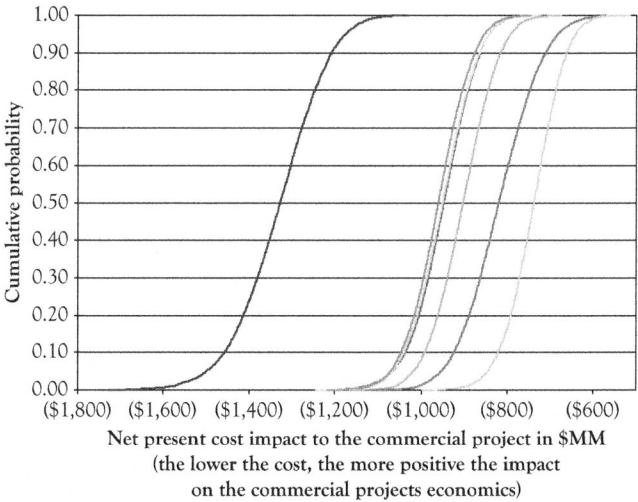

Exhibit 10-1. Net Present Cost of Different Plant Strategies

and we specifically designed this strategy to accommodate the technology we expected to commercialize in the coming years. The "Flexible Plant" property and buildings would be designed in such a way as to leave room for the next-generation product manufacturing processes, but we would not purchase any of the associated equipment until technical requirements and specifications had been fully developed and associated proof-of-performance testing had been completed. The other item to note is that we have previously argued that the strategy with the lowest risk (as determined by qualitative assessment) should also be the strategy with the lowest cost. We observe that this is not the result that we achieved and the explanation is that the absolute lowest cost strategy worked for a technology that had not yet been developed or tested. The Flexible Plant strategy, which did meet our project timing requirements was the next lowest cost alternative. So to proceed with the current project objectives, the firm made an executive decision to take on more risk.

This is all we really wanted to discuss with respect to decision framing. Once again, decision framing is all about using a tool to help determine a path forward to take a decision that is not able to be taken in the near term for any variety of reasons. It is not meant to be precise, but rather, to provide direction. In tying the conversation back into R&D and supply-chain development, one can now see the necessity of keeping the R&D group involved in the supply-chain development process from a technology point of view, but also, keeping the contracting and procurement group involved from a supplier point of view. In our case, the plant ownership and operatorship issue opened a whole new series of questions with regard to who was most suitable. To answer this question, we revisited the table presented in Chapter 2 to determine where the leverage points existed with respect to the firm operating a manufacturing plant. We then performed additional analysis to determine if constraints existed in finding suitable operating companies, analyzed the type of relationship that we would potentially have with an operating company, developed a go-forward strategy for the selected operator, and then war-gamed that strategy to test its viability. Our answer was to do it ourselves, at least at the start of the overall commercial project. Once we were well into the overall commercial project and had moved to the next-generation technology, we would then consider other options as to plant ownership and operatorship. By building our own manufacturing plant, we captured all the learning curves, we protected all the intellectual properties, we guaranteed that we would have the lowest total cost of ownership, we minimized our total risk exposure presented by the technology, and we had a single, constant and stable demand customer—ourselves.

CHAPTER 11

War Gaming and Table Topping Your Strategies

At some point during your supply-chain development program, it will become important to test some of the strategies that have been developed in as near a "real-world" situation as possible. War gaming and table topping are two excellent methods for receiving feedback regarding the potential success of your strategies. We have to admit, these two activities were extremely fun to do and were extremely valuable to us as we continued to formulate our strategies and develop our tactical plans.

Keep in mind that the technology was still being developed, supplier relationships with the R&D team were mostly contractual in nature, numerous change orders existed for various parts of the technology, and our suppliers seemed to be fairly content with our orders as they represented additional and unexpected revenue. Yet we knew that unless we could develop some sort of risk/cost sharing scheme with our suppliers and do more to engage our suppliers with our project, there was little hope of achieving significant cost reductions in this area. So let's talk about the tools.

What Are They?

War gaming is a very tactical tool that we used to test an individual strategy for one supplier, in a controlled environment, to see how it would hold up under simulated, real-world conditions. We did engage a consulting company to assist us with the effort of designing and conducting the game for one supplier that we were interested in and thought that we may have a long-term relationship with. Game results were then used to further refine our strategy to engage this supplier.

Table topping, on the other hand, is a different simulation exercise and consists of a consolidated review of all suppliers, strategies, and tactics that would be deployed to ensure that our technology arrived at the right place, at the right time, and at the right price. We also reviewed why a particular strategy was chosen to engage a supplier including the associated transportation and logistics strategies. This exercise was particularly beneficial in ensuring alignment with everyone on the team and brought an additional benefit as all the elements of the exercise were on display and review for everyone to see and comment on, particularly from folks who were not directly involved in the work being performed, such as R&D. The R&D group was able to see the impact of forward-looking statements made from their department to suppliers, and understand how some statements could be very misleading and result in the commercial team being unable to accomplish goals and objectives on the supply-chain side of the house. We will not spend a lot of time on table topping as it is akin to trying to describe how to play chess, that is, one knows all the individual moves that a piece is allowed to make, but putting those moves together in such a way as to win the game is extremely difficult to describe.

We will now speak to the war game design, conduct and lessons learned, and then follow that discussion with a review of the tabletop exercise.

The Actual War Game

The war game design effort took approximately eight weeks to accomplish. See Exhibit 11-1, where LT means Leadership Team. As previously noted, we did hire a consulting company to assist us in the design of the game and to perform the fundamental research required for the creation of briefing books. We selected a current and preferred supplier of a critical component of the technology based on the supplier relationship that had been developed by the folks in R&D. Over the course of our product development, two other suppliers had developed similar components, which were under evaluation by our R&D department for potential use in our product. The war game focused on how we would initially engage the preferred supplier, then would fast-forward two to three years into the project life cycle to test our strategy, and then finally looked about five years ahead to determine if our strategy could stand the test of time. The following section outlines the game design.

Firm LT and SCM (procurement)

Firm commercial team

Firm teams
- Develop strategies to engage with single source and multiple source suppliers
- Negotiate through contracting
- Engage in execution phase with suppliers
- Determine exit strategy

Control team
- Oversees wargame play
- Reacts for all others
- Introduces external shocks
- Judges overall move success

Negotiation

Component requests and deliveries

Teams communicate with each other to take actions, negotiate, make alliances, and strike deals

Control

Control is comprised of 3–4 consultants plus 1–2 firm staff

Supplier 1—current supplier

Supplier 2—competitor

Supplier 3—competitor

Supplier teams
- Identify objectives, priorities
- Develop strategies to engage as single source and multiple source suppliers
- Take actions to achieve strategy negotiate, make alliances, and strike deals
- Brief decisions and rationale to all other teams after each move

Wild card (i.e., other suppliers, firm corporate actions, etc.)

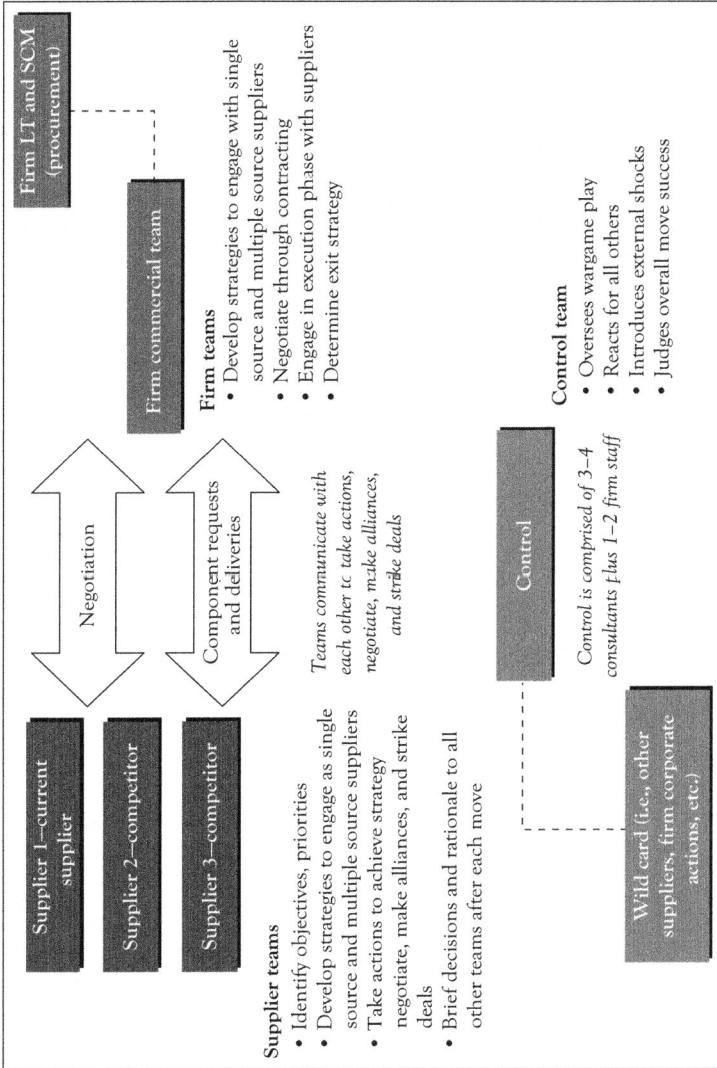

Exhibit 11-1. War Game Design

War Game Design

At the start of the game, the current supplier strategy that had been developed by the R&D team was used as the starting point for the commercial team. This relationship primarily focused on issuing purchase orders for purchased parts. The firm's overarching goal was to improve supplier performance and minimize supply chain risk. See Exhibit 11-2.

The game was limited to three suppliers that had been identified through the efforts of the R&D team. The firm's high level view of each of these suppliers is shown in Exhibit 11-3.

During the war game, suppliers would negotiate with the firm to obtain contracts for purchased components. Then, as the war game

Exhibit 11-2. Supplier Engagement Value Drivers

Overall cost	Product quality	Supply reliability	Relationship
Clearly achieve cost targets	High product quality	Supply chain response times	Intellectual property protection
Capture learning curve synergies	Minimal performance variations	Supply chain forecast accuracy	Exit rights
Year on year cost reductions	No transportation related failures	Vendor managed inventory	Willingness and ability to invest in capacity expansions
			Partner in innovation
Overall objective: Improve supplier performance and minimize risk through effective contract strategy, terms, and conditions			

Exhibit 11-3. High-Level Qualitative Assessment of Suppliers

	High-level performance perception			
	Technology	Quality/ Reliability	Capacity	Price
Supplier 1	passed both electrical and mechanical tests	some issues developing during performance trials	new plant is under capacity and can provide ~3M parts annually	~$26/part at 1M/year, >30% margin
Supplier 2	passed electrical tests (mechanical tests in progress)	N/A	plant can provide ~180K parts annually	~$35/part at 1M/year after capacity expansion, >30% margin
Supplier 3	passed electrical tests (mechanical tests in progress)	N/A	European facility can provide about 200K parts annually	~$60/part at 1M/year after capacity expansion, >30% margin

moved forward in time, various situations would be introduced to determine how the firm's commercial team would respond. See Exhibit 11-4.

To start the game, the commercial team started with the basic strategy of issuing purchase orders to obtain components. The commercial team's value drivers are summarized in Exhibit 11-5. The commercial team was also provided a letter from Supplier 1 outlining Supplier 1's key business drivers as shown in Exhibit 11-6.

Before going any further, it is important to note that a fairly significant effort was undertaken to prepare a briefing book of each supplier. This effort took between four and six weeks to complete, consolidate, and align to ensure sufficient information was available to the various commercial team members assuming roles as supplier teams 1, 2, and 3. The briefing material was provided to the team members approximately one week in advance of the war game. Each supplier team was then tasked with "homework" to get together and formulate their individual strategy in preparation for the war game. Supplier teams were not allowed to

Exhibit 11-4. War Game Moves

Move 1 qualification	Move 2 negotiation	Move 3 commercialization	Move 4 execution

• Areas to be tested
  – Supplier 1 engagement strategy
  – Negotiation strategy
  – Agreement terms and conditions with Supplier 1
  – Supplier relationships
• Key focus on single source supplier relationship
	• Areas to be tested
	  – Multiple supplier engagement strategy
	  – Incentive alignment
	  – Business allocation model
	  – Negotiation and contracting process
	• Key focus on business allocation and protection of intellectual property
		• Areas to be tested
		  – Responses to disruptions
		  – Supplier relationships and exit strategies
		  – Learning curve value
		  – Cost and reliability implications
		• Key focus on maintaining leverage on suppliers during project disruptions and capturing the learning curve
			• Areas to be tested
			  – Negotiation with suppliers under new scenario
			  – Incentive alignment
			  – Business allocation model
			• Key focus on learnings on contract negotiations under new set of conditions

Exhibit 11-5. Commercial Team Value Drivers

Key firm commercial team requirements
• The firm wants Supplier 1 to develop technology and capacity
• The firm never wants to be obligated to order parts as a condition of an alliance
• The firm wants the ability to terminate an alliance at any time
• The firm wants total visibility into part cost

Exhibit 11-6. Supplier 1 Starting Position

Supplier 1's key expectations
• Strategic partnership and preferred supplier relationship
• Major portion of supply contract (~80%) of the "component business"
• Mutual protection of intellectual property through two-way nondisclosure agreement
• "Open Book" relationship possible if gross margin is guaranteed

negotiate anything in advance with other supplier teams or to be made aware of whom the other suppliers were. In addition, each supplier team was given the status and results of any testing of their components that had been completed in the "real world" by the R&D team. The contents of the briefing books were as follows:

- Supplier strategic goals and objectives
- Products, applications, and geographic markets
- Risk profiles with respect to financials, business, and operations
- All financials
- Strengths, weaknesses, opportunities, and threats (SWOT) analysis with respect to the supplier being able to meet the firm's requirements
- The supplier's competitors, customers, and suppliers
- "Big picture" process maps with regard to basic production processes
- Cost structures
- Manufacturing locations.

War-Game Chronology

Exhibit 11-7 is a high-level summary of the war-game chronology included just to give an idea of the pace and the pressure under which the exercise was conducted. The actual "play-by-play" is contained in the Appendix. All communications between player teams and control were by e-mail.

Results

So what was the outcome? To be sure, the firm did not do nearly as well as what was expected and many lessons were learned that would need some

Exhibit 11-7. War Game Summary

Day 1	Key moves, issues, events
Hour 1	Commercial Team and Leadership Team unable to get aligned on critical supplier issues
Hour 2	Leadership Team direction to R&D personnel to quit talking to supplier. Commercial Team pace of negotiations is too slow
Hour 3	Leadership Team advises Commercial Team of project acceleration. Commercial Team provides incorrect quantities to suppliers and desires 100% access to supplier financial information, unable to agree to Non-Disclosure Agreement Terms and Conditions
Hour 4	Previously agreed to price has been raised significantly to meet acceleration requirements but without necessary volume. Commercial Team brings in two other suppliers for a bid meeting as they are unable to determine price and volume requirements from the current supplier
Hour 5	Supplier 1 walks out of negotiations due to heavy-handed approach by Firm, Supplier 1 CEO wants face to face conversation with Leadership Team, proposals obtained from other 2 suppliers
Hour 6	Leadership Team meets with Supplier 1 CEO unknown to Commercial Team, reopens negotiations with Supplier 1, cost modeling of each supplier proposals
Hour 7	Further analysis of proposals and proposed allocation of business between Supplier 1 and 2 is developed
Hour 8	Firm agrees to pay more than negotiated price, identifies safety stock levels for participating suppliers, Supplier 1 attempts to purchase Supplier 2
Day 2	Key moves, issues, events
Hour 1	Supplier 2 starts acquisition of Supplier 3, realignment of Commercial Team by Leadership Team
Hour 2	Pilot project successful—now ramping to full Commercial Project, bid meeting for all suppliers, Supplier 1 has no desire to negotiate but will attend bid conference, Commercial Team unaware of any tension with Supplier 1, proposals received from Suppliers, Firm Board of Directors (BOD) inquiry to Leadership Team as to problem with supply chains
Hour 3	Supplier 2 acquires Supplier 3, Supplier 1 anticipating major reduction in product sales and directed to aggressively engage in negotiations with Firm, Commercial Team complains to Control Team about pace and stress of game, Commercial Team request to Supplier 2 regarding new capabilities, capacities, strategies, etc. reiteration of project commercial requirements to Commercial Team
Hour 4	Control Team intervention with Commercial Team lack of progress with Supplier 1 in negotiations, Supplier 1 strongly desires to negotiate with Firm
Hour 5	Identification of capabilities and capacities from Supplier 2, analysis of proposals using cost models
Hour 6	Supplier 2 advises Leadership Team of potential business ethics violations of Supplier 1, Commercial Team is aware of allegations but has not advised Leadership Team of them, Supplier 1 admits they have "sailed close to the wind in the past" but is no longer the case, Commercial Team negotiates deal with Supplier 1

action plans developed as the firm moved forward. War game analysis, major findings, and other findings are presented in Exhibits 11-8, 11-9, and 11-10.

The commercial team's strategy did not reflect how difficult it was for the firm to leverage its scale and scope in a seller's market. It also highlighted the importance of establishing a highly functioning, well-performing team to avoid unnecessary delays and confusion.

The war game also highlighted areas regarding the firm's internal decision-making process needing improvement and the need for better internal alignment.

Exhibit 11-8. War Game Analysis

The current supplier engagement strategy was not effective • Mismatch with constrained supply • Multiple supplier market options • Future volume and timing uncertainty	• Supplier 1 initially walked out of the negotiations, largely due to the firm's heavy-handed approach to negotiations (and clear misalignment with reality of supplier situation above) • Discussions with all the suppliers quickly stalled around several disagreements (e.g., refusal from the firm to commit to volume did not project a trusting image to the suppliers, request to have only a one-way NDA led the supplier to refuse to provide open book access to the firm) • Failure to focus on what the two parties wanted to get out of the deal (e.g. the Firm worked to secure reliable and competitive supply, suppliers desired to establish a longer term partnership beyond the transaction of providing components) which highlighted that the various parties were talking past each other
The Firm's overall approach to negotiations was too heavy-handed	• Strategy was ineffective • Firm image was damaged within the entire supply base
Once a more collaborative approach on both sides was taken: • Breakthroughs occurred • Negotiations proceeded and circumvented areas of disagreement	• **Volume commitment**: This was actually not a major issue for suppliers since most of the manufacturing costs were variable and a win-win exit strategy, including the compensation by the firm for committed expenses (Raw material, WIP), was acceptable to both parties • Sharing of IP can be mitigated by holding suppliers accountable to delivering learning curve price reductions without requiring the Firm to become engrained into the supplier manufacturing process • Overall, supplier relationships improved dramatically when both parties decided to start talking about what they agreed on and worked together to manage their points of disconnect (i.e., they agreed to disagree and find work-arounds) • Although Supplier 1 did not appear to object to being put in competition with other suppliers, the firm's immediate needs seemed to be properly addressed with a single/multi-location supplier, while longer term needs could involve alternate suppliers to drive technology breakthroughs
An agreement was finally reached	• Agreement was tested and deemed robust to handle a number of possible disruptions such as supply chain interruption, surge in energy costs and project cancellation • An attractive price for the firm was reached

	Mismatch description	Magnitude of mismatch	Real world evidence/Game observations
Buyers vs. sellers market	• LT perception that component is a commodity. Suppliers and possibly R&D thinks it is a unique product. Commercial Teams perception somewhere in between	4	• All three suppliers average well over 30% Gross Margin indicating it is "supplier's market". Diversity of application inherently lowers demand dependency on an industry • The Firm's Commercial Team objective function on Day One was to make Supplier 1 lose or "beat them into submission" however, Supplier 1 refused to do business with the Firm—"walks out" during negotiation
Customer indifference	• LT, Commercial Team and R&D are all unanimous in their thinking that "Our Firm is Big and Suppliers will do what we want." Supplier thinks this might be a new opportunity	3	• None of the suppliers represented has Oil and Gas either as its core customer base or their sole corporate focus. The Firm's potential business represents less than 5% of overall business for all suppliers • Diversification of the industry base and engagement with the Firm (as a new customer) were among cited reasons for potential interest
Supplier uncertainty	• The Firm "teases" suppliers with huge demand volume but high volume uncertainty. Supplier pushes for minimum volume commitment	4	• Variables like production targets, numbers of components required, and design specifications are driving risks to suppliers that they will assume only at a premium • All suppliers pushed for minimum volume commitment—which the Firm's Commercial Team accepted in the final deal negotiated with Supplier 1, but, which was against the policy laid out by the Firm's Leadership Team (LT) (also an internal alignment issue)

Exhibit 11-9. War Game Major Findings (key: 1 is low and 5 is high)

Exhibit 11-10. War Game Additional Findings

General area	Key theme	Observations
Substantial intervention from Control	Identified lack of understanding of the firm's commercial team had of the leadership team's overall objectives	• Commercial Team required strong stimulus to generate action • Direct intervention of Leadership Team to focus on a "deal" as opposed to optimizing
Teams struggled to bring to bear the various expertise of their team members	Failure to quickly achieve common objectives	• Confusing communications between Commercial Team and suppliers • Excessive time spent on discussing technical issues not significantly relevant to the need of securing a stable source of supply
Not an integrated team	Lack of understanding of overall business needs and how to operationalize them	• Need for action not balanced with need for analysis • Negotiations not driven with skill or purpose
Firm internal decision making slow and ineffective	Frequent and deep disconnects and frustrations between Leadership Team and Commercial team. Leadership Team really wanted two strategies; one for short term and one for long term. This was never understood by the Commercial Team.	• Management direction perceived as unrealistic • Commercial Team response was too slow • Multiple points of contact with suppliers caused supplier confusion • Commercial Team felt "sidelined" once they learned that supplier had access to Leadership Team—did not matter what the deal was since supplier could get any deal they wanted • Commercial Team tried to make long-term strategy fit short-term commitments
Firm's desire to keep options "open" was counter-productive	Value was destroyed by lack of action	• Commercial Team focus on crafting optimum business allocation based largely on price yet failing to secure a sound supply source for short-term project

The "top 3" things that the firm needed to start working on are shown in Exhibit 11-11 and recommended corrective actions are shown in Exhibit 11-12.

So you may be thinking to yourself right now that all these things should be self-evident and that any self-respecting supply-chain organization would have never had these issues. Well, here's the deal:

Demand management

- Variability in demand characteristics (specifications or prints, volume, quality/reliability requirements, etc.) need to first be stabilized and then managed better (stage gated) and communicated through a single channel. Suppliers have mentioned the need for the firm to better manage its demand via a single point of contact and improve working relationships
- *Supplier 1 team mentioned that working with the Firm was akin to designing to ever-changing specifications*

Negotiation

- The Firm's traditional "heavy-handed approach" will not work given the supplier's market condition and demand uncertainty
- Negotiations around pricing and underlying product economics need to be in the context of volume, timing etc.
- *Relationship was adversarial and supplier negotiations had a touch of arrogance. The Commercial Team focused on price, NDA, and delivery where as the suppliers engaged at the IP and relationship level–cooperative negotiations were not in place until the Control Team's forcing functions limiting the scenario to only two suppliers*
- *Supplier agreement was not able to be solidified until Day Two of the wargame—far exceeding expected timeline*

Internal & external communications

- Multiple points of contact with each supplier resulted in a fragmented knowledge base across different functions: R&D, Technical Optimization, Supply Chain, etc. There was anecdotal evidence of inadvertent sharing of the Firm's IP while working with suppliers ("suppliers know too much")
- *Disconnect between LT and Supplier 3 resulted in: a) LT thinking that $25 was the final price and b) Commercial Team awarding only 25% of the business to Supplier 1 despite LT's perception of them being a "blue blood" "premier supplier," worthy of 100% of business*
- *Supplier 1 wanted a single point of contact to minimize confusion*

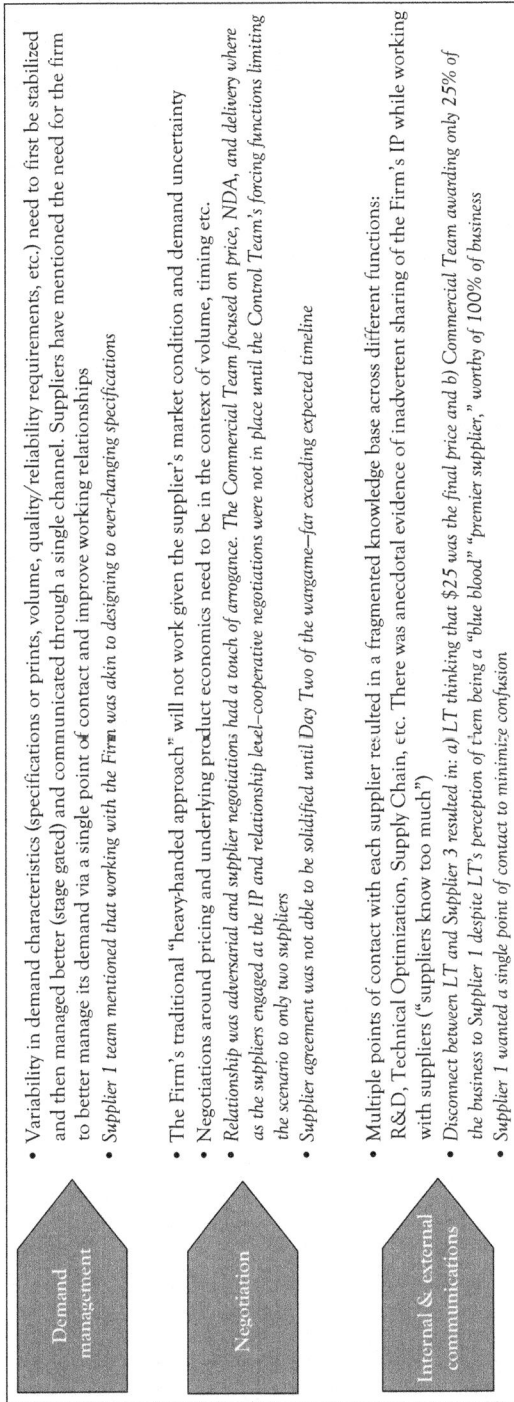

Exhibit 11-11. Top 3 Issues

Exhibit 11-12. Corrective Action Recommendations

Action item	Description	Objective
1.	Secure alignment with the leadership team around the need to approach potential suppliers in the context of a sellers market	Provide the Commercial Team the assurance that the Leadership Team is in line with them
2.	Establish cross-functional integration with adequate participation from affected internal stakeholders	Ensures an inclusive, informed, and strategic approach to supplier negotiations
3.	Reverse current mindset barriers and establish new paradigm based on single/few suppliers with multiple supplier market options vs. multiple suppliers with high Firm dependencies Differentiate between short-term and long-term goals and objectives, needs for immediate actions vs. long-term nurturing relationships Reevaluate needs for levels of integration with supplier	Design a realistic and robust strategy that avoids protracted negotiations yet leads to acceptable results for both Firm and suppliers

1. The firm's supply-chain organization was "too busy" solving the everyday contracting and procurement issues to be sufficiently engaged in really trying to work through how the supply chain would be developed out of R&D to commercialization. And to be fair, they were busy, as this group typically controlled contracts running on the order of $5 billion annually for the firm.

2. There was no recognition by the firm's leadership team, supply chain, commercial team members, or any of the supplier team members, of the implications of a supply-chain needing to be established in a *seller's market*. The firm's biases and heavy-handed approach to contracting and procurement, coupled with a "one-size-fits-all" mentality toward suppliers severely hampered the firm's strategy. While claiming to want to work with suppliers, the prevailing actions really indicated that the firm was simply in love with the *idea* of working with suppliers; otherwise, it was business as usual.

3. There was an overall failure of everyone to recognize that the supply chain would be a *constant and stable demand* supply chain. This issue

was never explored and had the commercial team appreciated the implications of this particular concept, significant negotiating power would have been at their disposal for long-term contracts.

4. Enough cannot be said about gaining internal alignment with regard to roles, responsibilities, approaches, and expectations.

Moving on to Table Topping

Whereas the war game is a very in-depth and tactical approach to what the firm wanted to do with a specific supplier, the table top exercise was a strategic approach to the overall supply chain and thus was much more focused on the "big picture." This exercise was geared toward identifying common themes, gaps in analyses, and so on, and less about specific details.

To start with, we obtained a large table size map of North America. The map was used to lay out all supplier locations for the non-commodity materials and components required to meet our needs. Plastic and wood materials, toys, and trucks were used to enhance the visual effect associated with the transportation network aspect of the supply chain. Other material prepared to assist in the exercise consisted of breaking down the overall supply chain into the individual chains associated with the major components of the final assembly. Each team member would then use the props and information they had developed to discuss the following minimum aspects of the supplier they were working with:

- Primary and alternate suppliers and locations
- Reported capacities and order lead times
- Material specifications, requirements, and starting forms
- Costs, order sizes, and frequencies
- Logistics providers and transport lead times
- Customs requirements
- Warehousing and any material handling requirements
- Primary risks
- Volume and pricing
- Safety stock and vendor managed inventory
- Status of non-disclosure, intellectual property, and other agreements

- Transportation routings and delivery schedules
- Transparency of production costs to the firm
- Business allocation among suppliers providing identical products
- Nature of the supplier relationship
- SWOT analysis of the supplier
- An evaluation of the supplier with respect to business risk presented to the firm should the supplier default
- Change management
- Learning curve capture.

As each team member reviewed and defended their analysis, assumptions were challenged, gaps were identified, and action items were assigned to ensure the most robust plan possible. At the end of the exercise, a series of "what-if" scenarios were introduced to test the overarching strategy of each team member with respect to contingency planning. Some of these "what-ifs" were:

- Liabilities and risks associated with project cancellation
- Supplier defaults
- Supplier mergers and acquisitions
- Significant project scope and/or timing changes
- Technology and/or component specification changes
- A change in the supplier relationship.

Final Remarks

We realize this has been a long chapter and appreciate your patience. We do wish to be clear about one thing – it is not necessary to use these tools for every aspect of your supply chain as you try to move your product out of R&D and into commercialization. One would really only want to do these to identify thematic areas of where gaps exist. For our particular team, and the effort we were engaged in, it was extremely important to "get it right" with this particular component as its failure would result in the failure of the entire finished product. Quite simply, it was the "Achilles Heel" of the technology and it had to be right. We did not get the supply-chain strategy right primarily because of our biases toward our suppliers and a fundamental misunderstanding of the seller's market that prevailed. In addition, we had a total lack of appreciation for what the constant and stable demand aspect of the project could do for us in terms of negotiation with suppliers. We know that you will do better.

CHAPTER 12

Putting It All Together

As in any book of this type, there are usually more than just a few questions that the text has had a tendency to generate. While perhaps we have outlined the "big ticket" issues that need to be addressed to get started and some ways on how one might accomplish these tasks, we would be absolutely remiss if we did not caution the reader that the "devil is in the details." Definition and clarity are of utmost importance every step along the way. Our purpose here was to forewarn and thereby forearm the reader, hoping and trusting that the reader will not get "forearmed" by the supply-chain development activities they are engaged with.

Understanding the magnitude of the project, its impact on world commodities, your companies' project drivers, the value drivers of those companies chosen to participate with you, and not being stymied with analysis paralysis are absolutely critical to the success of your efforts. Studying the commodity market, understanding how and why one would or would not participate in supplier networks, taking decisions with respect to make versus buy, knowing when it is appropriate to pursue low-cost country sourcing, developing strategic supply-chain models, and mitigating supply chain risks are critically important also. But in the grand scheme of things, and in the language of decision-framing, these are issues that are more tactical, not fundamental. Tackling tactical decisions before having clarity on fundamental decisions simply leads to increased levels of frustration and the tendency to suffer from analysis paralysis.

Is there a "12-step" process? Well, of course. The question is how many times do the steps need to be repeated to get the results that you need? Exhibit 12-1 summarizes the key points of each step as the supply chain is developed for new products emerging from the R&D function.

Exhibit 12-1. 12-Step Process for Successfully Developing Supply Chains for Products Emerging from R & D

Step	Scope	Key Points to Address
1	Supplier Landscape Analysis	1. Clearly determine the extent of any correlations between materials, industries, and geopolitics 2. Know what is a commodity and what is not and where the constraints are at in commodity processing that drive price volatility 3. Understand commodity market "drivers" 4. Be able to identify if operating in a "customer" market or a "suppliers" market
2	"Make" vs. "Buy"	1. Must be absolutely clear on "who" can do "what", both internally and externally to the firm 2. Determine leverage points for both "make" and "buy" decisions 3. Determine the nature of supplier relationships that will exist across all aspects of the product lifecycle 4. Define 2 to 3 high-level strategies to start working with and begin "high-level" qualitative and quantitative analysis
3	Low-Cost Country Sourcing	1. Must be absolutely clear on "who" can do "what", both internally and externally to the Firm 2. Must clearly have excellent insight into cost advantages and Intellectual Property issues 3. Must have sufficient awareness into regulatory environment, tariffs, dues, etc.
4	Intellectual Property Analysis	1. Is it needed? 2. Keep the legal folks involved
5	Supplier Network Analysis	1. Clear definition on "Gives" and "Gets" 2. Clear understanding of nature of supplier network complexity 3. Understand if operating in a "supplier" market and associated implications
6	Accommodating Design Changes	1. Integrate R & D stage gate processes with supply chain work practices 2. Allow ample time for supply chain to perform due diligence 3. Adopt industry best practices for new product development
7	Learning Curves	1. Understand what learning curves are for and determine if they should be used 2. "Line of sight predictions are hazardous"
8	Risk as a Measure of Total Cost of Ownership	1. Clear definition on all risk factors, weighting factors, and scores 2. Bias analysis 3. Clear understanding of results

9	Cost Modeling	1. Start strategically 2. Understand how cost model results can be used to influence suppliers
10	Decision Framing	1. Clear definition on decision question 2. Develop robust strategies 3. Develop high-level economic model that can be used to differentiate between the strategies
11	War-Gaming and Table Topping	1. Understand the differences and the applications 2. Utilize results to clarify engagement strategies and add clarity to tactical plans
12	Periodic Review of Results from Each Step	1. Life changes and need to stay on top of things

We are sure that if you follow the process as we have discussed, you will have great success in establishing the supply chain for products emerging from R&D. We wish you the absolute best of luck in "developing a world-class supply chain for a brand-new product that is going to change the world."

Before letting you go for good, we do feel a moral obligation to inform you that the 2008–2009 global economic and financial crisis ultimately caused an indefinite delay to the supply-chain design project. The team was disbanded, many team members were relocated within the firm while others left the firm altogether. The project was finalized, documentation completed, and stuck on the shelf.

CHAPTER 13

Conclusion

So you may be wondering a little bit about the appropriateness of all this work if you are not trying to change the world like we were. We believe that the sequence of work activities would still be appropriate; however, the depth of analysis for each of the work activities would differ. Exhibit 13-1 is merely a suggestion of the depth of the work activities based on project size.

We trust that you have had an enjoyable read and thank you for picking up this book to begin with. If what we have written has helped you with some of your supply chain issues, then we consider this book to have been worth all of the time and effort expended. And remember that the most effective way to do it, is to do it. May the force be with you!

Exhibit 13-1. Work Activities by Project Size

Work activity	Project size		
	<$100M	$100–$500M	>$500M
Supplier landscape analysis	X	X	X
Make vs. buy analysis		X	X
Low-cost country sourcing			X
Intellectual property analysis	X	X	X
Accommodating design changes		X	X
Learning curve analysis			X
Risk as a measure of total cost of ownership		X	X
Cost modeling	X	X	X
Supplier networking analysis	X	X	X
Decision framing		X	X
War gaming			X
Table topping	X	X	X

EPILOGUE

Back in Business!

Moving forward a few years, we are happy to report that at the time of this writing, the supply-chain design project is back in business. After several years of being dormant, the economic and technical dimensions of the project are being updated, revised, and improved to deal with the present day market conditions. Remember that "next generation" technology we discussed? How we did not expect it to be ready for three to four years after we started with the technology currently on the table? Remember how painful the discussion was on incorporating learning curves into project economics and jumping from one product learning curve to the next product learning curve? What about the ideas of supplier networking and partnering? Or how to deal with intellectual property protection? All of these are now back in play, perhaps not to the same scale as what we were engaged in, but nevertheless taking on greater priority in the overall project discussion. Unfortunately, due to confidentiality considerations, we cannot say anymore and will simply leave it to your imaginations.

.

APPENDIX
War-Game Chronology

Start of Day 1

Time	To/From	Communication
0859	Control to all players	Everyone on line: Note, all communications were by e-mail and were copied to Control
0903	Control to Commercial Team	Query status of strategy alignment with Leadership Team (LT)
0903	Commercial Team to LT	Query on volume requirements and margin expectations
0909	LT to Commercial Team	Two scenarios: use industry standards for margin requirements
0924	Control to Commercial Team	Query status of Commercial Team/LT alignment
0934	LT to Commercial Team	Query status of Commercial Team/Supplier 1 talks
0941	LT to Commercial Team	Commercial Team summoned to LT to provide alignment and negotiation mandate Authors' note: 40 min into the game and the Commercial Team is *summoned* to the LT. This would be a recurring theme throughout the game
1019	Supplier 1 Board of Directors (BOD) to Supplier 1 CEO	Query on status of Firm negotiations
1030	Supplier 1 CEO to Supplier 1 BOD	Firm wants cost structure, no risk, and identifies potential projects in mid-East and China, Supplier 1 wants two-way non-disclosure agreement (NDA), perhaps use a third-party negotiator, no contract in place
1042	LT to Commercial Team	Approved to negotiate per mandate and principles
1043	LT to R&D	Stop talking to Supplier 1, Commercial Team is single point of contact as opposed to LT and R&D Authors' note: The issue of R&D speaking to suppliers tremendously aggravated not only the Commercial Team, but also suppliers. Clear indication of internal misalignment issues and conflicting roles and responsibilities
1048	LT to Commercial Team	Provide status, negotiation pace is too slow
1051	Commercial Team to LT	Point brief on Supplier 1 negotiation position
1053	Corporate Headquarters (HQ) to LT	Update on project timing expectations, query on cost and schedule risk using typical contracting and procurement strategies

Time	To/From	Communication
1056	Commercial Team to Supplier 1	Request for proposal (RFP) for NDA
1057	LT to Commercial Team	Desires to clarify positions based on 1051 information (time stamp)
1102	Commercial Team to LT	Query on alternative technologies
1103	LT to Commercial Team	Notification of project acceleration requirements
1105	LT to Commercial Team	Query to Commercial Team on cost and quality of alternative technologies
1116	LT to Commercial Team	Query R&D status of alternative technologies
1120	Supplier 1 to Commercial Team	Invite to Supplier 1 HQ, pursue NDA, and third-party negotiator
1123	LT to Commercial Team	Summons for update
1127	LT to Commercial Team	Query on Supplier 1 cost
1128	LT to Commercial Team	Query on Supplier 1 cost
1130	Commercial Team to LT	Query on alternative technologies
1131	LT to Commercial Team	Stick with existing technology
1136	LT to Commercial Team	Query on price – seems too low for little project
1136	Commercial Team to Supplier 1	Supplier 1 notified of pilot and provided Request for Quotation (RFQ)
1137	LT to Commercial Team	Query on acceleration of pilot project
1137	Commercial Team to LT	Confirmation of $25 cost
1138	LT to Commercial Team	Reiteration of project and acknowledge $25 per piece price
1139	Commercial Team to LT	Confirmation of $25 per piece price for 100K pieces
1141	LT to Corporate HQ	Response to cost and schedule concerns, identification of risks, and magnitude of component costs on total assembly costs
1141	Supplier 1 to Commercial Team	Ready to negotiate, waiting on NDA

Time	To/From	Communication
1142	LT to Commercial Team	Re-query on quantity requirements
1144	Commercial Team to Supplier 1	Request for quote
1144	LT to Commercial Team	Clarify expectation that Commercial Team should have clear understanding of volume requirements Authors' note: A fundamental calculation error occurred in that the Commercial Team incorrectly determined quantities required. Seems like a simple math problem, but it really wasn't; however, the LT is correct in their expectation
1145	LT to Commercial Team	Copy of response to Corporate HQ
1149	Commercial Team to LT	Query for project requirements
1150	Commercial Team to LT	Miscalculation of quantity requirements (Control note: reported values are too low and issue is not recognized by Commercial Team – LT believes there is a problem with quantity requirements)
1151	LT to Commercial Team	Request for clarification on price for small project
1151	Supplier 1 BOD to Supplier 1 CEO	Query on Firm fast track of pilot projects
1152	LT to Commercial Team	Clarification on quantity
1153	Commercial Team to Control	Additional resources requested
1155	Supplier 1 CEO to Supplier 1 BOD	Still negotiating
1156	Commercial Team to Supplier 1	Reiterate 100% access to financial information
1157	Commercial Team to LT	Request further clarification on project requirements
1157	Control to Commercial Team	No additional resources available
1159	Supplier 1 BOD to Supplier 1	Query and analysis of negotiation situation
1204	Commercial Team to Supplier 1	No NDA at this time, place order for 60K at $25 each
1205	Supplier 1 to Commercial Team	Price is $45 each and will not respond to internal finance discussions due to no NDA clarity around third-party negotiator, commitments with other customers and so unable to meet

Time	To/From	Communication
1209	LT to Commercial Team	Copy of response to Corporate HQ – reiteration of $25 price per piece
1209	Supplier 1 to Commercial Team	Supplier 1 will not support $25 price premise and volume is below minimum requirement. Will not respond to RFQ. Authors' note: This should have been a huge red flag to the Commercial Team, and it was not communicated for some time to the LT. Bait and switch? No, ill-defined specifications coupled with lower than expected volumes
1212	Supplier 1 CEO to Supplier 1 BOD	No support for Firm's request due to amount of risk Firm is placing on Supplier 1 and no NDA or clear specifications
1219	Commercial Team to Supplier 1	Supplier 1 has given three different prices. What's going on?
1251	Commercial Team to Supplier 1, Supplier 2, and Supplier 3	Invitation to Supplier bid meeting at Firm location. Authors' note: A near 100% increase in price caused the Commercial Team to bring all suppliers into a joint supplier bid meeting where the Firm laid out all specifications, requirements, volumes, and timing
1254	Control to Supplier 2	12 months and $2M capital to switch manufacturing process
1301	Commercial Team to Control	Waiting on response from suppliers to attend bid meeting
1315	Supplier 1 to Commercial Team	Desire to meet; request for agenda
1320	Supplier 1 CEO to Supplier 1 BOD	Pursuing further research to truly determine Firm and other companies' true needs
1324	Supplier 1 to Commercial Team	Accept meeting. If Firm provides clear scope of work, then Supplier 1 can provide 60K parts at $38 each within 20 weeks
1327	Supplier 1 press release	Supplier 1 has released project manager and quality specialist for previous line of business and are pursuing other businesses to fill the gap
1327	LT to Commercial Team	Supplier status update query
1329	Supplier 3 to Commercial Team	Desire to discuss joint development proposal for new material. Quote provided for 50K–200K at $80 each with delivery in 90 days
1332	Supplier 1 BOD to Supplier 1 CEO	Query for clarification on what is to be done for "today" not "years" from now
1341	Supplier 1 CEO to Supplier 1 BOD	Walked away from negotiation – able due to Firm only allowing ½ of negotiation party to participate. Justification that 3% of Supplier 1 business does not warrant this kind of treatment with Firm driving a one-way street. Interaction dynamics must change to allow any sort of deal to be made. Authors' note: This was an incredible development. The Firm's heavy-handed approach to negotiations coupled with a clear misunderstanding and misconception of Supplier 1 business environment led to the walk-out

Time	To/From	Communication
1345	Commercial Team to LT	Concerned about Supplier 1 walkout. Their attitude toward meeting Firm's needs is challenged. Proceeding with negotiations with other suppliers to meet immediate needs
1345	Supplier 2 to Commercial Team	Cannot support 60K units at $25 each but can support 25K/mo at $40 each with ability to ramp up to meet Firm's requirements with no assistance from Firm
1347	LT to Commercial Team	Query on why Supplier 1 walked out
1350	Supplier 1 CEO to Supplier 1 BOD	Initiating contact with Firm counterpart and advise of disrespect that Supplier 1 has received from Firm and failure to recognize that Supplier 1 is a leader in their field. Must have mutual respect. Current level of negotiation is inadequate
1353	Supplier 1 BOD to Supplier 1 CEO	Other impending business issues that Firm may be able to assist us with in the future. Reiterate need to keep dialogue open given the frustration level
1353	Supplier 1 CEO to LT	Request face to face meeting to discuss inadequate negotiation with Firm (not up to industry standards)
1354	Supplier 3 to Commercial Team	Reiterate joint development proposal for alternative material to reach price targets requested by Firm. Offer of 60K pieces for cost of 55K (5000 free pieces) at $22 each
1356	Supplier 1 CEO to Supplier 1 BOD	Query about other issues affecting business
1358	LT to Commercial Team	Query to Commercial Team regarding why Supplier 1 CEO desires to meet with LT Authors' note: So the LT wants to know why the CEO of Supplier 1 wants to have a meeting unbeknownst to the Commercial Team. This was a bit problematic since the LT had directed everyone that the Commercial Team was the single point of contact but if they do not agree to meet with the Supplier 1 CEO, they may have never discovered the poor treatment Supplier 1 was receiving at the hands of the Commercial Team.
1401	LT to Supplier 1 CEO	Will respond shortly
1401	Control to Commercial Team	Alternative material will be allowed for long-term assembly development but not for short-term project
1403	Supplier 1 BOD to Supplier 1 CEO	Response to other impending business is that so much of business is dependent on their #1 customer, however, still need to pursue as that status is about to change

Time	To/From	Communication
1405	Commercial Team to Supplier 3	Query on length of time to qualify new material. Query for cost breakdown between 200K and 2M pieces/yr. Query about willingness to reduce costs in short run in return for potential future business. Looking forward to proceeding with Supplier 3
1406	LT to Commercial Team	Second query on background information for meeting with Supplier 1 CEO
1409	Commercial Team to LT	Willing to listen to reasons for walkout
1409	Supplier 1 CEO to Supplier 1 BOD	Market analysis complete – other opportunities aside from Firm with other companies
1412	Supplier 1 BOD to Supplier 1 CEO	Emphatic direction to keep dialogue with Firm open
1412	LT to Commercial Team	Since there is no background information from Commercial Team to LT, the LT will meet with Supplier 1 CEO and get back to the Commercial Team Authors' note: The Commercial Team did not deliberately stonewall the LT, but, it was quite clear the Commercial Team did not understand the importance and potential implications of the meeting
1413	LT to Supplier 1 CEO	Let's meet
1418	Control to Cost Modeling Team	Analyze Supplier 1 for 60K pieces @$38 each, Supplier 2 for 250K pieces @$40 each, and Supplier 3 for 200K pieces @$80 each Authors' note: The Cost Modeling Team was responsible for determining the appropriate amount of volume to be allocated per supplier in accordance with the cost and risk models that had been developed. Those models are discussed elsewhere in this book.
1422	Commercial Team to all suppliers	Setup individual supplier meetings times
1424	LT to Commercial Team	Summons to meet Authors' note: Did not even want to be around for this discussion!
1428	Control to Cost Modeling Team	Clarification of monthly quantities
1430	Supplier 3 to Commercial Team	Four months to qualify alternative material in lab followed by field testing

Time	To/From	Communication
1433	Supplier 1 CEO to Control	Desire to have third-party negotiator/mediation team
1441	Supplier 3 to Commercial Team	Revised quote for current material including scale-up quantities
1442	Supplier 1 CEO to LT	Thank you note for meeting, standing by to receive Commercial Team, pursuing third-party negotiator, reevaluate ability to drive down costs, reaffirmation of ability to meet quality and delivery requirements, request future meetings to be more aligned with mutual goals
1442	Supplier 1 CEO to Supplier 1 BOD	Reopening Firm negotiations
1444	Information from Cost Modeling Team to Control	100% of business should be given to Supplier 1, Supplier 2 can come on as second supplier as volume goes up, Supplier 3 should receive no business
1446	Supplier 1 CEO to Supplier 1 BOD	Recommendation to pursue buyout of Supplier 3 North America Division
1447	Supplier 1 BOD to Supplier 1 CEO	Query for purchase of Supplier 3 – show the numbers
1451	Supplier 1 BOD to Supplier 1 CEO	Will not support third-party negotiations
1453	LT to Supplier 1 CEO	Continue working with Firm Commercial Team
1454	Supplier 1 CEO to LT	Pursuing third-party negotiation to meet with Commercial Team
1458	Supplier 1 BOD to Supplier 1 CEO	BOD will not support third-party negotiations
1500	Supplier 1 BOD to Supplier 1 CEO	Summons to report to the BOD. Desired negotiator is a long-term supporter of Firm and represents a conflict of interest
1513	Corporate supply chain specialist to LT	Hand calculations show that there is some confusion regarding quantity. Order quantities appear to be too small to support project. Authors' note: A recurring theme
1518	LT to Control	Confusion surrounding quantity of material being ordered. Quantities are too small to support project
1535	Supplier 3 to Commercial Team	Confusion on quantity and timing of order. Request for clarification for 4M parts
1546	Supplier 3 to Commercial Team	Request for exploring pass through of a portion of Firm's energy credits at a tier 2 level to help drive down costs through energy savings

Time	To/From	Communication
1551	Supplier 2 to Commercial Team	Cost for 60K is $37 each with delivery in 2 months. Will not accept any Firm capital. Supplier 2 will fund production switchover. Exit cost to Firm will be $4M. Cost for 250K = $28.5, 500K = $27.5, 1M = $26.5, 4M = $24.75. All forward IP to be jointly owned and subject to licensing and royalty agreements
1622	Control to Cost Modeling Team	Proposed business allocation is 75% Supplier 2 and 25% Supplier 1
1630	Commercial Team to all suppliers	Information on next bid meeting times
1631	Cost Modeling Team to Control	Based on quotes given, Supplier 2 should receive 61% of business and Supplier 1 39%
1643	Supplier 1 to Commercial Team	Meeting acceptance
1644	Supplier 3 to Commercial Team	Cost for current material is $48 each, 60K of alternative material is $ 30 each, with lead times of 75 and 35 days, respectively
1650	Supplier 2 to Commercial Team	Supplier 2 accepts order for 170K units at $37 each
1704	Control to Cost Modeling Team	Analyze cost to Firm with respect to 75%–25% split
1708	Control to Cost Modeling Team	Supplier 2 allocation is 170K out of 200K and Supplier 1 is 56K for total of 226K pieces
1712	Cost Modeling Team to Control	Based on order above, Firm will pay ~$10,000 more/month and service level will drop from 99.6 to 99.1% due to Supplier 2's inability to deliver parts on time (basically a 75%–25% split vs. the 61%–39% split which is the most optimum). Firm is leaving money on the table by not following recommendations from their own business allocation model
1725	Cost Modeling Team to Control	Recommendation that Supplier 2 hold 5155 components as safety stock thereby raising service level to 99.9% and Firm costs would go down by ~10,000/month (a $20,000 swing from what was negotiated)
1740	Control to Cost Modeling Team	Query for allocation if Supplier 1 cost had been $28 each

Start of Day 2		
Time	To/From	Communication
		Authors' note: Supplier 1 was unsuccessful in their attempt to purchase Supplier 3
0757	Cost Modeling Team to Control	Response for Supplier 1 components at $28 each and current demand is 55%/45% for Supplier 1. If demand increases by 50%, then the allocation changes to 81%/19% for Supplier 1
0826	Supplier 2 to Control	Query regarding Supplier 2 acquiring Supplier 3
0832	Commercial Team to LT	Query on large project scope. Date? Quantities?
0836	LT to Commercial Team	Summons for face-to-face meeting
0843	Commercial Team to Supplier 3	Request for quote for between 200K and 1.4M components
0844	LT to Commercial Team	Project scope defined. Desire minimal cost, 100% reliability, perfect quality, corporate alignment with Firm business principles, and multiple sources
0907	Control to all	Please provide negotiation schedule
0910	Commercial Team to all suppliers	Pilot project has been successful – now ramping for big project be prepared to discuss delivery schedules. RFQ must address: Ability to carry safety stock, year-on-year cost reductions, . Quantities (annual), how many times per year unplanned disruptions are experienced and how they are addressed.
0914	Commercial Team to all suppliers	Invite to bidders conference
0917	Supplier 2 to Commercial Team	Supplier 2 will attend
0917	Supplier 1 to Commercial Team	Supplier 1 will attend, but no negotiations will occur
0918	Commercial Team to Supplier 2	Appointment time details
0919	Commercial Team to Control	No desire to change to plenary session. Commercial Team is in Control
0923	Supplier 2 to Commercial Team	Confirming appointment
0925	Commercial Team to Supplier 3	Notice of appointment time

Time	To/From	Communication
0928	Commercial Team to Supplier 1	Notice of appointment time
0930	Supplier 1 to Commercial Team	Clarification desired on appointment time being for Supplier 1 or Supplier 3
0932	Commercial Team to all suppliers	Notification of deadline for all quotes
0933	LT to Commercial Team	Query to Commercial Team regarding tension with Supplier 1. Offer to assist in getting things patched up. Any talking points that need to be conveyed?
0935	Commercial Team to LT	Unaware of any tension with Supplier 1. Thanks for offer. If there is something we need to know then please let Commercial Team know. Authors' note: Unbelievable huh? Not only did the LT meet with the CEO of Supplier 1, they mentioned nothing of the meeting to the Commercial Team during their follow-on meeting and instead chose to push past the issue. The Commercial Team is still blissfully uninformed of how they are being viewed by Supplier 1
0936	LT to Commercial Team	Just responding to comments from the scene settings for the start of Day 2
0942	Supplier 1 to Commercial Team	Response to RFQ: Supplier 1 can carry reasonable safety stock. Cost reductions can be taken into account Annual quantities—1.4M Experience disruptions—unscheduled shutdowns per year of 2 weeks 0.2M start at $38 and drop to $28 0.4M start at $38 and drop to $27.5 0.6M start at $38 and drop to $27 0.8M start at $38 and drop to $26.5 1.0M start at $38 and drop to $26 1.2M start at $38 and drop to $25.5 1.4M start at $38 and drop to $25 start up is $38 for first 8 months
0945	Supplier 1 to Commercial Team	Request for clarification on meeting time

Time	To/From	Communication
0947	Commercial Team to Supplier 1	Clarification sent
0948	Supplier 3 to Commercial Team	Response to RFQ: 200K at $43, 400K at $33.5, 600K at $28.5, 1M at $27, and 1.4M at $23.5. These prices are based on Firm providing the energy required 4.00/component. Lead-times: first 150,000 pieces after 2 months, thereafter 150,000 each month. Safety stock: Price includes 1 month safety stock. Quality: our internal reject rate is < 1.0% included in our pricing. Maximum capacity available is 2M components/year. Additional 1M pieces capacity can be build @1.55M. Capex Terms include: Prices are Firm for the first year, and will be indexed thereafter based on Terms & Conditions mutually agreed. Learning curve savings will be shared 50/50 – 10 years contract. Termination: Firm pays for all "work in progress" and safety stock upon 3 days cancellation notice
0950	Commercial Team to Supplier 3	Summons for negotiation

| 0954 | Firm Corporate HQ to LT | Wanted to get a quick update on the business. Understand that there have been some project delays due to supply-chain issues. No desire to have a repeat of similar events experienced by other projects as related to supply-chain issues. How are things going with your suppliers? Is there anything I can do to help? Looking forward to your soonest response. |

Time	To/From	Communication
0957	LT to Firm Corporate HQ	All business requirements identified, will meet with team to provide update
0959	LT to Commercial Team	Summons for update
1001	Supplier 3 to Supplier 2	Confirmation of offer details, 10X EBITDA plus parachute clauses for executives. Authors' note: Supplier 2 and 3 reach a deal where Supplier 2 purchases Supplier 3
1002	Supplier 2 to Commercial Team	Summons for update
1002	Supplier 2 to Commercial Team	Response to RFQ: Supplier 2 wants $250K for a 50K unit capacity. 6 months lead time for any capacity increase. 12 month lead time for technology change
1002	Supplier 1 BOD to Supplier 1 CEO	We have received information from our primary customer that they are anticipating a 75% reduction in requirements from Supplier 1. It is unclear at this time whether the reduction is due to a reallocation as allowed by our existing contracts or due to other world events. Either way, the BOD is expecting a significant business hit. Please advise us to the nature of your negotiations with Firm and what progress we will be able to make to minimize the business impact
1004	Supplier 2 to Supplier 3	Agreement to terms of purchase 10X EBITDA plus clauses
1007	Supplier 3 to Supplier 2	Deal on purchase
1008	LT to Commercial Team	• Ensure collaboration between Firm and suppliers [be careful not to use solely the conventional approach]... show respect ... better negotiator will occur Authors' note: Finally! • Keep under time lines must meet our business needs/requirements
1009	Supplier 2 news release	Supplier 2 has purchased Supplier 3: Significant increase in stock prices today due to a huge acquisition. Supplier 2 acquired Supplier 3 for undisclosed price, increasing their *dominant* position in this market segment. Quote from CEO, "We need the second facility to support new opportunities. We have plans to significantly increase the R&D efforts on alternative technology that could provide significant cost reductions in our products."

Time	To/From	Communication
1013	LT to Firm Corporate HQ	Here is the update: • We are talking with three suppliers, RFQ has been sent. Prospective suppliers fully understand our needs and requirements. • We are expecting to make decisions shortly [as per agreed timeline] • Next step in the process will be more collaborative than previous conventional approaches. • We are striving lowest total cost of ownership and long-term relationships that can continually drive cost down As you know, this is long-term contract where quality and delivery are paramount. *We feel it important to work in cooperation with our prospective suppliers*
1015	Supplier 1 CEO to Supplier 1 BOD	Positive meeting with Firm – waiting results
1016	Supplier 1 to Control	Concern about not allowing the Commercial Team sufficient time to respond
1033	Supplier 1 CEO to Supplier 1 BOD	Notification of intention to pursue other industries and announce new product offerings. Don't worry
1038	Commercial Team to LT	Thanks for update to corporate. Advise LT as to takeover of Supplier 3 by Supplier 2
1040	LT to Commercial Team	Aware of press release, good opportunity for all, new technology is not field tested
1041	Commercial Team to Supplier 2	Request for overview of Supplier 2's strategic plans
1044	Supplier 2 to Commercial Team	Supplier 2 and Supplier 3 offers are now withdrawn. New offer forthcoming shortly
1045	Commercial Team to Supplier 2	Request for clarification on future manufacturing facilities, supply chain, and potential for additional savings
1046	Commercial Team to Supplier 2	Request for new RFP
1052	Supplier 2 to Commercial Team	Request for slight delay for meeting
1056	Commercial Team to Supplier 1	Request to meet regarding Supplier 2 press release
1058	LT to Commercial Team	Reiteration of requirements as a result of merger and acquisition: *This is what we want:* • Minimal cost component [supplier development/learning curve, cross functional team to work on problems, collaborative] • Perfect quality • 100% reliability [delivery, no disruption] • Corporate alignment with our suppliers [Firm's business practice] • Desire multiple sources [defined as multiple companies or multiple manufacturing facilities] Please continue to commit to getting the deal complete... focus on collaboration to optimize our long-term profitability and relationship

Time	To/From	Communication
1058	Commercial Team to LT	Negotiation team meeting with Supplier 1. Waiting on new proposal from Supplier 2 There is a problem now in that the pricing doesn't match the quantities being handed out. Assuming Supplier 1 could be convinced to use the lower pricing and based on both runs, put Supplier 1 price at 27.50 (their 400–600K price), Supplier 2 at $37 (their 200–400K price) and Supplier 3 at $30 (their 600K price). There is an inherent problem with Supplier 2 capacity. At 25% of our current demand and having the same reliability and yield as everyone else, it puts them out of the game because their price will be too high
1059	Cost Modeling Team to Control	Allocation results: There is an email in which Supplier 2 wants $250K to build 50K in capacity. I assume the 50K capacity is per month and that means they have a 600K capacity per year. Supplier 1 has a 1.4M/year capacity. Supplier 3 said 2M/year. We need roughly 1.14M components per year. Therefore, to begin the model pick everyone's 1.2M/year price. Supplier 1 was tricky because they start at $38 and drop to $25.5. Therefore, run the model twice, once at $38 for Supplier 1 and once at $25.5. At $38 for Supplier 1, $22.2 for Supplier 2, and $25 for Supplier 3, will result in a service level of 99.933%
1104	LT to Commercial Team	Status of discussions with Supplier 1, reminder of time constraints, do we need face to face?
1105	Commercial Team to LT	Negotiation delayed due to Control meeting with Supplier 1 Authors' note: Control was required to make a direct intervention into the Commercial Team with respect to the continued lack of progress in negotiating with Supplier 1 and what appeared to be what could be termed as a "loss of big picture" accident with respect to the purpose and intent of the war game
1114	Control to Cost Modeling Team	Supplier 2 has purchased Supplier 3
1133	LT to Commercial Team	Summons for update
1134	Commercial Team to LT	Update: bullets on our recent meeting with Supplier 1: • Very amicable and constructive • Achieved lower costs than our initial estimates • Willingness to work with Firm on lowering costs through lean approach and energy • Credit proposal • Agreed to work on the safety stock • Supplier 1 recently opened discussions with local authorities on tax and energy incentives • Plan to move production to new facility

Time	To/From	Communication
1134	Supplier 1 CEO to Supplier 1 BOD	Response to Control / BOD discussion. In light of the recent discussion between CEO and the Chairman of the Board, we would like to offer a more robust understanding of our internal plan, which will meet all requests to stay engaged with Firm but also maintain current revenue base. We would like to start with some current facts:
		1) By our primary customer reducing demand by 75% by the end of the year, we will experience a drop in our current 77% revenue piece of the pie. We currently hold that of the 77%, 16% of this based in a sub-industry and we will maintain that contract
		2) Due to capacity constraints and a current lack of cash flow, we cannot increase output at any of our locations nor can we go above a production of more than 1.44M components per year
		3) We just ended our second set of negotiations with the Firm Commercial Team and amicably answered all given questions and preempted them for other concerns we thought the Commercial Team might have
		4) Supplier 2 buying Supplier 3 does not have major effect in our market segment; however, there will be an effect in the overall market. More to follow
		Our current plan includes the following:
		1. Cost structure for delivery of .8M to 1.4M annual pieces ranges from $26.50 to $25 during the ramp of stage.
		2. We have incorporated learning curve, process improvement, and energy reductions as part of an estimated further cost reduction to be reviewed after the ramp up process is winding down.
		3. We are currently re-evaluating our initial cost per unit
		Overall business strategy
		1. Replace lost revenue with possibly the following:
		a. Energy project developed through the partnership with Firm.
		b. Moving another specialty product into a full product line, which will introduce a new market segment product and introduce us to a new segment.
		We feel above proceedings are the way for us to maintain our current profit

Time	To/From	Communication
1135	LT to Commercial Team	Summons for update
1138	Supplier 1 to Commercial Team	Currently revising proposal. Will have ready shortly
1143	Commercial Team to Supplier 1	Query of plant capacity, Mean Time Between Failures (MTBF) and Mean Time to Repair (MTTR)
1149	Supplier 2 BOD to Supplier 2 CEO	Please clarify capabilities
1150	Commercial Team to Supplier 2	Request for final proposal
1150	Supplier 1 to Commercial Team	MTBF and MTTR data supplied
1159	Supplier 2 to New Supplier 2 BOD	Update on capacity: 2.25M units
1200	Corporate HQ to LT	Another company has developed an alternative technology that also appears to use same material and products as ours. What is impact on Firm?

1201	Supplier 1 to Commercial Team	Our pro-rated credit plan incluces the following considerations.
		1. We will not be using projections for the rebates, but will instead be utilizing historical data.
		2. We will be plotting daily per part cost versus time (every 8 hours) which will incorporate the different shift costs as well.
		3. By implementing the following we will be able to have quantitative numbers to use:
		  a. Actual energy costs
		  b. Resource allocation changes
		  c. Logistical move to Supplier 2 and savings it renders
		4. By implementing the following and utilizing our expert team composed of lean qualified and International Standardization Organization (ISO) qualified experts we will be able to give qualitative analysis for the following and generate an agreeable rebate
		  a. Monthly Kaizen events
		  b. Weekly 5S events

1201	Supplier 2 BOD to Supplier 2 CEO	Clarify actual capabilities
1204	Supplier 1 to Commercial Team	Supplier 1 team in meeting – please notify when can we meet

Time	To/From	Communication
1207	Commercial Team to Supplier 2	Response to RFQ requested
1208	Supplier 2 to Commercial Team	Response: 200K at $43, 400K at $33.5, 600K at $30, 800K at $28.5, 1M at $27, 1.2M at $25, and 1.4M at $23.5. These prices are based on Firm providing the energy required @ $4.00/component. Maximum capacity available is 2M components/year. Delivery Schedules • Ability to carry safety stock: We'll do it; want to store on-site at Firm's location and want real time inventory visibility • Year on Year (YOY) cost reductions: 1% reduction a year for 3 years • Quantities (annual): 2.25M per year. No exit penalty. • How many times per year do you experience unplanned disruptions and how do you address such disruptions? Safety stock will alleviate any problems due to disruptions. Alternative Material Prices per unit – these are *estimates*. 1M at $17, 1.2M at $15, 1.4M at $13. Firm providing the energy required @ $2.00/component. Timing: pending Firm testing and approval
1209	Control to Cost Modeling Team	Forward Supplier 2 capacities and cost quote
1210	Supplier 2 to Supplier 2 BOD	No capacity for another change to production process at this time
1211	Supplier 1 CEO to Supplier 1 BOD	Communicate desire to pursue alternative energy industry
1214	Supplier 2 to LT	Forwarded article regarding allegations of improper business practices on the part of Supplier 1. Request for meeting
1220	Cost Modeling Team to Control	Here is what happens first at the 1.2M price for both, then the price adjusted to reflect actual quantities and then what happens when Supplier 3 gets 80% and Supplier 2 gets 20%. If that happens, Supplier 1 needs to hold over 78K components in inventory. Supplier 2 buys Supplier 3. Supplier 1 at $25.5, Supplier 2 at $25
1250	LT to Commercial Team	Forward information on misconduct allegations of Supplier 1 to Commercial Team

Time	To/From	Communication
1257	Commercial Team to LT	Acknowledge awareness of issue and express concern over risks. Will be reevaluating Supplier 2 proposals
1257	Supplier 2 BOD to Supplier 2 CEO	Query on actual capabilities
1259	Commercial Team to LT	Query on proposed meeting with Supplier 2
1300	LT to Commercial Team	Query on impact of competitor development of alternative technology
1305	Commercial Team to LT	Some awareness of work, no awareness of technologies, need help from R&D
1307	Commercial Team to LT	Will continue negotiations with Supplier 1 subject to LT approval
1310	LT to Commercial Team	• This information on alleged misconduct places us in an awkward position [i.e., Firm's business values] • Partnering in a company that practices illegal activity can damage our reputation – somehow, in past conversations, we didn't realize the seriousness of these allegations. Perhaps, a miscommunication on our part • However, due to the project schedule timelines, we need to proceed to finalize contracts • There needs to be clear clauses articulating any other allegations, negative press that will damage our reputation; we reserve the right to terminate
1311	LT to Commercial Team	Focus on current needs and proven technology
1314	LT to Commercial Team	Plan to meet with Supplier 2 – provide status of allegation and any suggested talking points
1317	LT to Supplier 2	Summons to meet
1318	Commercial Team to LT	As earlier discussed, we were aware of what really amounts to allegations and acknowledgement by Supplier 1 that they have sailed close to the wind. Supplier 1 has addressed the issue in their annual report and has committed to address this issue in a businesslike manner. In our negotiations, we have stressed the need for all suppliers to meet Firm's business principles and this will be part of the contract under negotiation. In short, we believe that we can proceed with the negotiation and will articulate clauses that address Firm's exit from the contract should allegations be proven
1323	Commercial Team to LT	Keep Supplier 2 focused on eventual use of future technology and stress that current cost structure will not work for us. Eager to support them
1328	LT to Commercial Team	Meeting with Supplier 2 now, explaining projects and timelines, alternative material is premature

Time	To/From	Communication
1344	Commercial Team to LT	Draft contract arrived at with Supplier 1: Firm Commercial Team – Supplier 1 Contract • Quantity Firm Commercial Team commits 120K components per month on average Minimum monthly requirement of 66K/mo to hold pricing scheme Firm to provide demand visibility for inventory management • Timing Day 1 is initiate Purchase Order Day 90 – First FOB destination point – 120K components Day 120 – Next FOB has 120K + 120K as safety stock. Inventory to be at Firm location on consignment • Price * 120K components per month - $38 unit price for the first 4 months - $25 at day 120 - Firm Commercial Team and Supplier 1 will jointly collaborate on learning curve impacts - Target price of $18/unit including learning curve impacts • Quality * Supplier 1 will meet all specification quality requirements * Supplier 1 agrees to third-party quality improvement professional • Delivery * Supplier 1 agrees to deliver on time 100% meeting Firm's acceptance criteria Safety stock level commitment * 1.5 months of safety stock (180K components) • Penalties * Supplier 1 induced - Failure to meet quality - Failure to meet delivery - Third-party inspection of received parts

Time	To/From	Communication

1344 (cont.)	(Contract continued)	* Firm induced
		  - Change of technology
		  - Firm would compensate
		  - Safety stock, inventory, WIP
		  - Raw material on order
		  - Energy savings commitment
		• Firm business principles
		* Firm has the right to extract itself from the contract should Supplier 1 find itself through legal process unable to deliver parts
		• Intellectual Property
		  * Firm has no interest in knowing Supplier 1's business process other than what is required for process improvement/cost reduction

1350	LT to Commercial Team	Need more detailed language on termination clauses – focus on any legal proceedings or financials that are detrimental to Firm's reputation
1355	Commercial Team to LT	Amended contract to include above
1357	Supplier 1 CEO to Supplier 1 BOD	Finalized negotiations with Firm. Contract renegotiation is annually for the next 5 years
1357	Control to all	Wrap-up everything. Plenary session in 3 minutes
1359	LT to Commercial Team	Proceed with Supplier 1
1400	Control to all	War game is over – proceed to plenary session

Index

CPSIA information can be obtained at www.ICGtesting.com
Printed in the USA
LVOW04s1627060715

445137LV00020B/1244/P

9 781606 493953